MW01014072

Revolutionary Era Monmouth County

The Townships and Villages
of Revolutionary Monmouth County

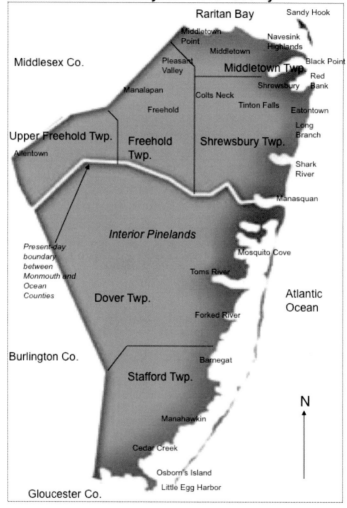

THE AMERICAN REVOLUTION
IN
MONMOUTH
COUNTY

The Theatre of Spoil and Destruction

MICHAEL S. ADELBERG

THE
History
PRESS

Published by The History Press
Charleston, SC 29403
www.historypress.net

Copyright © 2010 by Michael S. Adelberg
All rights reserved

Cover images: New Jersey Militia as portrayed by reenactors. *Photo by Gina Provenzano, Monmouth Battlefield State Park, Manalapan, New Jersey, 2008*; Drawing of the Monmouth County Courthouse by Carrie Swift, circa 1880. *Courtesy of the Monmouth County Historical Association, Freehold, New Jersey. Gift of Mrs. Rulif V. Lawrence, 1932.*

First published 2010

Manufactured in the United States

ISBN 978.1.60949.001.0

Library of Congress Cataloging-in-Publication Data

Adelberg, Michael S.
The American Revolution in Monmouth County : the theatre of spoil and destruction /
Michael S. Adelberg.
p. cm.
Includes index.
ISBN 978-1-60949-001-0
1. Monmouth County (N.J.)--History--18th century. 2. New Jersey--History--Revolution,
1775-1783. 3. United States--History--Revolution, 1775-1783. I. Title.
F142.M7A329 2010
974.9'4603--dc22
2010037823

Notice: The information in this book is true and complete to the best of our knowledge. It is offered without guarantee on the part of the author or The History Press. The author and The History Press disclaim all liability in connection with the use of this book.

All rights reserved. No part of this book may be reproduced or transmitted in any form whatsoever without prior written permission from the publisher except in the case of brief quotations embodied in critical articles and reviews.

CONTENTS

FOREWORD

During the eighteenth century, Monmouth County was one of the most ethnically, culturally and religiously diverse counties in the province of New Jersey. Its prosperous rural economy supported a comparatively large population. Numerous waterways permeated the county's extensive coastline, contributing to a lively coasting trade, and its strategic situation opposite the "gateway port" of New York City meant that it enjoyed the benefits of participation in the larger Atlantic economy. There is suggestive evidence that even in the colonial period local politics in Monmouth were volatile.

With the outbreak of the Revolutionary War, these factors—cultural diversity, relative prosperity, proximity to New York and a legacy of contentious politics—combined to make Monmouth an anxiety-ridden, violence-prone region. For seven years, the British headquarters in New York and its outposts exerted a destabilizing influence on counties such as Monmouth that were within the military frontier. Both imperatives of survival and the lure of profits drew people of all political persuasions to participate in contraband trade with New York, a nagging problem that was never effectively suppressed.

Monmouth County's wartime experience provides ample evidence of "asymmetric warfare." The county arguably suffered more civil strife over a longer period than any comparable region in Revolutionary America. It bred some of the war's most zealous Patriots, as well as some of the most ardent opponents of the new political order. In the midst of these polarized factions existed the majority, comprising the rest of the political spectrum: moderates, trimmers, neutrals and the apathetic. Late in the war, the crescendo of retributive violence gave birth to two opposing organizations, one Patriot and one Loyalist, both of which institutionalized the law of "an eye for an eye."

For more than two decades, Michael Adelberg has devoted himself to studying the fascinating social laboratory of Revolutionary Monmouth County. The database he compiled on more than sixty-five hundred county residents is an amazing achievement. His body of work not only describes events but also places them within a conceptual framework. Specifically, he has applied the methods of quantitative analysis to the very difficult problems of explaining allegiance and relative amounts of suffering. Overall, Mr. Adelberg has made a significant contribution to understanding the social history of the Revolutionary War on the homefront in New Jersey. It is a great benefit to researchers to have his past scholarship, together with new insights, published by The History Press in *The American Revolution in Monmouth County: The Theatre of Spoil and Destruction*.

David J. Fowler

ACKNOWLEDGEMENTS

S o many people have been helpful to me in researching the American Revolution in central New Jersey that I cannot possibly acknowledge them all. But a few have been mentors and advocates and must be noted. From a scholarly perspective, David Fowler "discovered" civil warfare in central New Jersey during the American Revolution, and everything I have written owes him a nod. This book goes down a path he blazed. For more than twenty years, the Monmouth County Historical Association has patronized my research, and its support undergirds this book. I extend heartfelt thanks to Lee Ellen Griffith, Laura Poll, Bernadette Rogoff and Glenn May for all their encouragement over the years. Gary Saretzsky at the Monmouth County Archives and Garry Wheeler Stone at Battlefield State Park have shown great generosity in sharing their resources and taking an interest in my work. Others, including Peter Micklaus (formerly of the New Jersey Historical Commission), Betty Epstein (New Jersey State Archives), Kathryn Grover (former editor of *New Jersey History*), Bruce Vandervort (editor of the *Journal of Military History*), Paul Axel-Lute (Rutgers University Law Library, Newark) and Professor Lawson Bowling (Manhattanville College), have provided guidance and inroads that kept me going.

Whitney Tarella and the staff of The History Press have been a pleasure to work with from day one, and I extend my sincere thanks to The History Press for conceiving of a collection of linked essays on the American Revolution in Monmouth County as the basis for a satisfying book. Finally, I extend great thanks to Judy Adelberg, my mother, for her diligent copyediting and necessary hectoring of the overwritten early drafts of this book. If this book is a great read, it is because of her. If it is not, it is because I did not heed all of her advice.

INTRODUCTION

In a December 1778 letter to General George Washington, New Jersey governor William Livingston earnestly requested assistance to defend the areas of his state facing British-held New York City. In the letter, he referred to the exposed Monmouth shoreline as "the theatre of spoil and destruction."

Livingston was particularly concerned by the situation in Monmouth County. By late 1778, the county had already been the scene of more turmoil and clashes than most localities endured over the course of the entire war, and warfare in Monmouth County would carry through 1782, more than a year after the Battle of Yorktown (supposedly) ended hostilities. Over the course of the war, Monmouth County hosted well over one hundred skirmishes and battles. It was New Jersey's most violence-prone locality and was among the most violence-prone localities anywhere in the new nation. The Sandy Hook Peninsula, on the county's northeast tip, was occupied by the British longer than any other piece of land anywhere in the Thirteen Colonies, and the county hosted one of the war's largest battles: the Battle of Monmouth, June 28, 1778. More than 10 percent of the county's men suffered bodily harm, and an estimated 50 percent of the county's families suffered tangible harm to a person or property during the war. Governor Livingston was not overstating the case when he called the county "the theatre of spoil and destruction."

———

Revolutionary Monmouth County, New Jersey (comprising the present-day counties of Monmouth and Ocean), occupied the eastern part of central New Jersey. It was among New Jersey's larger, wealthier and more populous counties and was also among the new nation's more diverse regions, inhabited by significant numbers of English (Anglicans, Quakers and Baptists), Scotch-Irish (Presbyterians), Dutch (Dutch Reformed) and a sprinkling of other Europeans. More than one-tenth of the population was African American, with large numbers of both slaves and freedmen. The county was divided commercially: the southern and westernmost parts were economically tied to Philadelphia, but the majority of the county was tied to New York.

Despite this, the county was profoundly rural by any modern standard. Monmouth County's entire population was between twelve and fifteen thousand—fewer people than attend a single NBA basketball game today. Even its largest villages—Freehold, Middletown, Shrewsbury, Middletown Point and Allentown—did not support any of the amenities, industry or culture associated with large towns or cities. The county had only one school, which met in a personal residence near Freehold. Enormous stretches of land, particularly along the shore and the swampy, pine forest interior, were uninhabited. Travel within the county was difficult. There were few roads besides those linking the northern villages, and the county's ports were too shallow for large vessels. In the entire county, there were perhaps twenty men with college educations—handfuls of ministers, attorneys and physicians. These men (and wealthy men in general) were afforded great respect from their peers, but there were limits to this deference, and many of the county's prewar squires suffered a fall of wealth and status during the war.

The Revolution brought new men to prominence and created a freer, fairer government. It also created opportunities for settling old scores and making money in new endeavors (locals speculated wildly in privateering and salt-making). The level of violence, change and opportunity within the county forced the people who lived there to be locally preoccupied. In the hundreds of documents surviving from Revolutionary Monmouth County—letters, petitions and military and court records—state-level affairs are only rarely mentioned, and national level affairs are almost never mentioned.

Monmouth County was part of a military frontier that stretched around British-held New York City from central New Jersey into southern New

York State. Across the military frontier, each side launched numerous raids against the other. The Continental and state governments had little ability to protect the people of these localities, and this forced locals to adopt coping strategies that included cooperating with both sides and embracing armed vigilantism. Even before raid warfare began, locals were split in their loyalties. Some Patriots (they called themselves Whigs) wholeheartedly supported independence and made great sacrifices for the new government, but more simply complied with the new laws and did only what was required. Some Tories (they called themselves Loyalists) risked life and property to join the British military and oppose American independence, but more stayed on their farms and weathered the war as "disaffecteds"—people whose opposition to independence was evident but not so extreme as to risk prison or property confiscation. Many people switched sides (sometimes more than once) based on short-term self-interest, self-preservation or disappointment with the side they had previously supported.

In no part of the military frontier was civil and irregular warfare more intense than in Monmouth County. Here, the American Revolution was especially confusing and norm wrenching. In the later years of the war, it was also dirty and brutal. Whigs inside the county fought against Loyalist raiders coming over from New York, Loyalist partisans within the county and covert disaffecteds whose true loyalties were hidden. But Whigs also came to blows with other Whigs. The annual county elections were often marred by violence, and intense factional rivalries dominated local politics. Loyalists were also divided between those who put themselves within the formal British command structure and its rules and those who became vindictive and ungovernable, even by the British. The war increased violent crime and paved the way for a great deal of opportunistic plundering masquerading as military operations. This contrasts sharply with the popular conception of the American Revolution as a contest between the Continental and British armies in which both the sides and goals of the war were fairly clear. In Monmouth County, the larger war between the full-time armies mattered, but on most days for most people, the local war mattered far more. This book is devoted to the key aspects of this local war.

1

An Overview of the American Revolution in Monmouth County

M onmouth County had a history of violence and tumult that began long before the Revolutionary War. In 1701, Monmouthers rioted to free the captured pirate Moses Butterworth and captured the governor and attorney general who had come to the county to oversee Butterworth's trial. By mid-century, Monmouth County's numerous small ports—Middletown Point, Shrewsbury, Manasquan, Toms River—were harbors for smugglers engaged in illegal trade with Great Britain's enemies in the Caribbean. In 1765, when resistance to the hated British Stamp Tax mounted, dissidents in Middletown and Upper Freehold Townships established "Suns [sic] of Liberty" groups. A few years later, as the economic crises of the 1760s climaxed, Monmouthers rioted in 1769 and again in 1770 to close down the courts and prevent foreclosures on family farms for unpaid debts (a similar riot occurred in Essex County).

New stresses became evident in the 1770s. Trevor Newland and John Morris, the only two retired British army officers living in the county, led a small group of men in burning the home of Samuel Bennett; they were charged with arson. A British tea ship that was turned away from New York Harbor (following the Boston Tea Party) came across the harbor to Monmouth County but received no assistance from locals. It was then driven ashore on Sandy Hook. When the British closed down Boston Harbor, Monmouthers rallied to support the Bostonians. In 1774, Edward Taylor chaired a countywide effort that raised 1,140 bushels of rye and other provisions for the "suffering of Boston." In the coming months, Monmouth County, along with most New Jersey counties, established committees of observation and inspection to oversee a boycott of British goods and committees of correspondence to coordinate dissent with other localities. Monmouth County elected and sent delegates to the New Jersey Provincial Congress (allied with the new Continental Congress) but also continued to elect delegates to the New Jersey Assembly (serving the royal governor).

The American Revolution started incrementally in Monmouth County. In late 1775, Captain Elias Longstreet raised a company of men from the county and joined the Continental army on its ill-fated invasion of Canada. But not all Monmouthers were Whigs (supporters of independence). Particularly in the three shore townships—Shrewsbury, Dover and Stafford—Quakers argued against war, and recently arrived British immigrants and most Anglicans maintained loyalty to their mother country. When Governor Dunmore, the royal governor of Virginia, declared that any slave of a rebel who assisted the British army would earn freedom, word spread quickly. Monmouth County's large African American population (more than 10 percent of the county's population) became restive. The first campaign of the county's new militia was against the county's own black population, not the British. For several months, Monmouth's largest township, Shrewsbury, altogether refused to establish a county committee to coordinate the boycott of British goods and was declared "separated" from the county by the committee at Freehold.

1776

In early 1776, a Continental army recruiting drive led by Colonel David Forman succeeded in raising over two hundred men from Monmouth County, and they marched off for New York in June. Meanwhile, British warships landed on Sandy Hook, established a base there and began intercepting vessels traveling from Middletown to New York. Despite numerous attacks in the coming years, the British did not give up the Hook until the end of 1783, so a piece of Monmouth County was held by the enemy longer than any other piece of land in any of the Thirteen Colonies. That same month, the militias in Freehold and Upper Freehold split into competing associations, both factions supporting resistance to British policies but differing in their views on independence. In June, anti-independence petitioners collected hundreds of signatures from Monmouth County.

An Overview of the American Revolution in Monmouth County

On June 29, 1776, a massive British fleet carrying twenty-five thousand soldiers landed at Sandy Hook and Staten Island. The sight of this powerful fleet emboldened Monmouth County's Loyalists and disheartened some of its Whigs. Sixty Monmouthers under John Morris, a former British army officer living near Manasquan, joined the British army. Other Loyalists—from prominent men with patronage positions in the New Jersey government to runaway slaves—turned "refugee" and joined the British. After receiving little state or Continental support, Colonel George Taylor, commanding the Monmouth militia facing the mighty British army, became disenchanted and started cooperating with local Loyalists. Colonel Samuel Breese, commander of the militia in Shrewsbury Township, resigned from the militia "owing to the backwardness of the people" and declared himself a neutral. Loyalists across the county asserted their allegiance to the British Crown.

On July 2, 1776, the same day that the Continental Congress debated a declaration of independence and the New Jersey Provincial Congress established a new state constitution, Monmouth County went into a state of confused insurrection. The Provincial Congress ordered 250 Burlington County Militia into Monmouth County to quell "a number of disaffected persons…preparing by force of arms to oppose the cause of American freedom, and to join the British troops." A few days later, a regiment of Pennsylvanians joined the fight at the direction of the Continental Congress.

Loyalist insurrections bubbled up and simmered down for the next several months, resulting in dozens of arrests and property confiscations but little bloodshed. The civility of this quasi civil war was dashed when Colonel David Forman's regiment of Continentals, raised from Monmouth and Middlesex Counties in the spring, returned home to crush the Loyalists once and for all. Forman made approximately one hundred arrests and sent the prisoners off to jail out of state (to Pennsylvania and eventually Frederick, Maryland) without trial. The arbitrary treatment of the Loyalists and alleged Loyalists escalated tensions within the county.

When Forman's regiment dissolved in early December 1776 (the men's six-month enlistment expired), the county's Loyalists rose up massively in a movement termed the "Tory Ascendancy" by locals. General William Howe, commanding the British army, was so impressed by the actions of the Monmouth Loyalists that he extended the winter quarters of his forces into western New Jersey, specifically for the purpose of "covering" Monmouth's emboldened Loyalists. Leading Monmouth County Whigs, including John

Covenhoven (the man who chaired the writing of New Jersey's constitution) and Lieutenant Colonel Thomas Seabrook, were captured and detained. Under duress, they signed loyalty oaths to the British. Loyalist refugees, now organized as the First and Second Regiments of the New Jersey Volunteers, returned home British soldiers. Loyalist elder statesmen were appointed commissioners for administering British "protections" to loyal citizens. Loyalist gangs retaliated against Whigs by confiscating their livestock, guns and wagons, ostensibly because these were items of military value. Public notices went up across the county, advertising the first general muster for the new (Loyalist) militia at Freehold on January 1. George Taylor, formerly the senior colonel of Monmouth County's Whig militia, was named colonel of the new Loyalist militia. As 1776 ended, Loyalists were in charge.

1777

Just as the Loyalists of Monmouth County were establishing a functioning regime, the British army retreated across New Jersey following the Continental army's surprise attack at Trenton. This opened Monmouth County to Whig counterattack. Within a few days of the Battle of Trenton, regiments of Pennsylvania and Delaware Continentals entered the western part of the county. On January 2, 1777, the 200-man newly mustered Loyalist militia clashed with 120 Pennsylvania Continentals. After a short battle, the Loyalists scattered, resulting in several battlefield deaths and loss of considerable supplies. The Continentals pushed east and further broke up Loyalist associations at Middletown and Shrewsbury. The Loyalist regime in Monmouth County was fully toppled by the end of January. Two weeks later, the newly embodied Whig militia, camped on the Navesink Highlands, was surprised by a regiment of British regulars, resulting in the death of 25 and the capture of 72 Monmouth Whigs. Monmouth County was very much at war.

Throughout 1777, Monmouth County did not have a functioning government. The Loyalists had confiscated county records. Key leaders were ineligible for their elected offices because they had signed British loyalty oaths or because they (illegally) held both military and civil government appointments. There was no mechanism for filling the open offices. The courts did not meet, and the county's annual election broke down into violent riot when Colonel David Forman (now also brigadier general in the New Jersey Militia) and his supporters showed up with arms and bullied voters into supporting the slate of candidates Forman favored. (The election was voided by the New Jersey legislature.) This was one of many abusive acts Forman committed as he claimed martial law authority, allegedly granted him by George Washington. Forman deported a number of Loyalist women, hanged a captured Loyalist without a proper trial, used troops under his command as private laborers at his saltworks and squabbled with another New Jersey Militia general. The reaction to Forman's excesses came from more even-tempered Whigs. The New Jersey Assembly summoned him to answer for his conduct and eventually censured him. Forman refused the summons and resigned his militia commission in protest. At the request of the New Jersey government, General Washington transferred command of Forman's Continental army regiment to Colonel Israel Shreve of Burlington County. The Continentals were ordered from the county in January 1778.

The excesses of Forman and his allies allowed Loyalists to maintain some amount of popular support. Almost two hundred Monmouthers enlisted in the Loyalist New Jersey Volunteers in early 1777, and entire neighborhoods, particularly along the shore, resisted mustering into militia companies and paying taxes. Illegal trade between Monmouth farmers and British-held New York flourished, earning the nickname "London trade." Loyalists based on Sandy Hook and Staten Island started launching vengeful raids into Monmouth County. They burned the Presbyterian meetinghouse at Middletown and captured its minister, Charles McKnight (he became fatally ill in prison); they plundered the home of Lieutenant Colonel Thomas Seabrook (during which Seabrook's son was badly wounded); and they overpowered a militia detachment and captured Captain John Dennis (he died in prison two months later). Colonel George Taylor, now a Loyalist, led a string of incursions into Monmouth County, resulting in skirmishes against the same men he had commanded less than a year earlier.

1778

After a relatively quiet winter, the raids began again. In early April, a large Loyalist raiding party landed at Manasquan and razed the massive Union Saltworks (co-owned by David Forman). Six weeks later, another large Loyalist raiding party landed at Middletown Point, where the raiders captured leading Whigs, committee chairman John Burrowes and Captain Jacob Covenhoven, and many others. The ineffective response of the

Monmouth militia to this incursion resulted in the court-martial of Major Thomas Hunn. Perhaps influenced by these and other incursions, the newly functioning Monmouth County courts issued a string of capital convictions against imprisoned Loyalists in early June.

Just as court concluded, the larger war once again intruded into Monmouth County. The British army, retreating from Philadelphia toward New York City, came into Monmouth County on June 25 and paused at Freehold on the twenty-seventh to gather its extensive baggage train (which extended twelve miles). The newly confident Continental army—bolstered by new recruits, European advisors and an alliance with France—came across New Jersey and engaged the British on the morning of June 28. In the daylong battle that followed, the Battle of Monmouth, both sides advanced and retreated before the lines hardened, and an artillery duel filled the end of the day. Despite a full day of combat, heat and dehydration claimed about as many lives that day as the actual battle. Monmouthers near Freehold spent much of that summer caring for the wounded, burying the dead and recovering from the arson and plundering of the armies. (The British army burned an entire neighborhood of homes near Freehold.)

With the British on the defensive, hemmed into New York City and diverting men and ships to fight the French elsewhere, privateering blossomed. Little Egg Harbor, just south of Monmouth County, became New Jersey's busiest port. A twelve-hundred-man British raid that October against the port demonstrated that the British could still strike and destroy any coastal target they selected. A Continental army regiment under Kasimir Pulaski was sent into southern Monmouth County to check the plundering. As the Continentals camped at night on Osborn's Island in the harbor, disaffected locals and Pulaski's own deserters guided the British to Pulaski's camp and watched as the Continentals were massacred. Meanwhile, Loyalist partisan gangs, started by Monmouth Loyalists who had deserted the harsh British army, formed along the shore. These gangs—known locally as Pine Robbers—engaged in a string of violent robberies against Monmouth Whigs. The most infamous of these partisans were eventually captured and killed, but most were not. They remained unconquered through the duration of the war. Reluctantly, General Washington committed soldiers to Monmouth County in an attempt to curb the London trade and provide support to Monmouth's vulnerable Whigs.

1779

Following a winter lull, raid warfare began in earnest in April 1779. Two raids against Tinton Falls, the only Whig stronghold near Sandy Hook, resulted in the loss of the militia magazine collected there, the capture of Shrewsbury Township's senior militia officers and abandonment of the village. The raiders, according to a witness, "seemed like wild or mad men" as they razed the village. These raids also demonstrated the weakness of Continental soldiers in helping with the county's defense. During the April 25 raid, the Continentals retreated without firing a shot, while the local militia heroically skirmished with the raiders throughout the day.

Loyalist anger rose with the confiscation and sale of over one hundred refugee estates in May. To Loyalists living in New York, the confiscation of their estates ended any chance of reconciliation with the rebels. The Loyalist estate auctions in Monmouth County were marred by accusations of collusion and corruption, fueling Whig mistrust of other Whigs. Rival Whig factions formed within the county between a radical bloc (mostly Presbyterians from Freehold Township) led by David Forman and Congressman Nathaniel Scudder and a more moderate bloc (mostly ethnic Dutch from Middletown and Shrewsbury Townships) led by Colonel Asher Holmes and Assemblyman James Mott.

The New Jersey government understood the stresses within the county. Governor William Livingston called for militia from other counties to march into Monmouth on many occasions, but the assistance rarely arrived, as leaders from other counties were generally unwilling to march their men into another county's quagmire. In May 1779, the state provided a more meaningful type of aid by funding a regiment of so-called state troops for Monmouth County. These men would be raised from the Monmouth militia but would function as full-time soldiers with state pay and supplies. State troops were reauthorized continuously through the end of 1782, a greater commitment of state support than offered to any other county. However, the state troops and militia were still not able to check the Loyalist raiders coming from Sandy Hook and New York or curb Pine Robbers and London traders operating within the county. The murder of Thomas Farr, the Upper Freehold tax collector, by a gang of Pine Robbers in October 1779 proved that any Whig—even those living thirty miles inland—was vulnerable.

1780

The year 1780 was, in many ways, the hardest one of the war for the people of Monmouth County. More Loyalist raids and clashes occurred in this year than in any other. The most effective were the half dozen led by "Colonel" Tye, a runaway slave from Shrewsbury Township who emerged as the leader of a group of African American Loyalists called the Black Brigade. Among other accomplishments, the Black Brigade captured Lieutenant Colonel John Smock, Assemblyman James Mott and Assemblyman Hendrick Smock, carried off dozens of head of livestock and penetrated fifteen miles inland to Colts Neck. Meanwhile, the London trader and Pine Robber gangs along the shore continued operating without any effective check. Excluding Toms River, where the local militia operated the privateer gunboat *Civil Usage*, there is little evidence that the shore villages supported the Whig war effort.

Inland, however, 1779 and 1780 were the years in which Monmouth's Whigs finally stabilized local government. Courts met regularly, taxes were collected in each of the townships (though only under armed guard in the shore townships) and a string of militia court-martials fined over two hundred men for delinquency. In the summer of 1780, the majority of the country's Whig leaders formed an extralegal group called the Association for Retaliation, committed to practicing eye-for-eye revenge for any damages inflicted on the group's nearly five hundred members. However, when the Retaliators began impressing the goods of people with no direct link to Loyalist incursions and the New Jersey legislature condemned the group for creating "disloyalty and disunion," Monmouth's more moderate Whigs dropped out.

At the October 1780 county elections, anger between the two Whig blocs boiled over. Forman's supporters again came to the polls with arms, and Forman-allied election judges closed the polls before many of the moderate voters from the far-flung townships arrived. When Assemblyman James Mott protested, Forman, by his own admission, "did beat, wound, and ill-treat" Mott in front of a crowd. The rivalry between the blocs also played out in the courts, where the leaders of the blocs frequently filed suits and countersuits against each other. The confiscation of a wagonload of John Holmes's (Holmes was from a prominent family of moderate Whigs) goods by Major Elisha Walton (a leading radical Whig) resulted in a nasty legal dispute that went to the New Jersey Supreme Court. The court, siding with the moderates, overturned the confiscation of Holmes's goods by declaring the confiscation process unconstitutional. It established the important legal principle of judicial review in doing so.

1781

The year 1781 replayed the themes of 1780. Loyalist raids continued, including a massive incursion of fifteen hundred British regulars and Loyalists in June. But the Monmouth militia and state troops showed growing competence in fighting back, even winning some of the skirmishes with smaller raiding parties. In one of these skirmishes, Congressman Nathaniel Scudder was killed while advancing with the militia against a raiding party. He was the only member of the Continental Congress killed in combat. Monmouth Whigs also received greater support from outside the county. The elite Continental dragoons of Major Henry "Light Horse Harry" Lee, the daring New Jersey privateer Adam Hyler and other privateers from New England made bold descents against Sandy Hook. Monmouth's Whigs also asserted more influence along the disaffected shoreline. A campaign that December resulted in the arrest and detention of thirty-seven London traders, including members of the prominent Woodmancy and Ridgeway families, officeholders in the Dover and Stafford Township governments. Retaliators continued to punish local disaffecteds, and the county elections were again marred by violence and allegations of coercion.

1782–83

Following the surrender of the British army at Yorktown (October 1781), the British went into a shell in New York City and began peace talks premised on American independence. But raid and irregular warfare did not slow down in and around Monmouth County. Along the county's southern shore, Pine Robbers consolidated into two large gangs under the leadership of John Bacon and mysterious "Davenport" (mysterious because the real identity of this person remains unknown to this day). In a pitched battle at Cedar Creek, the Pine Robbers routed the militia when locals joined in to support the Loyalists. Loyalist refugees in New York also consolidated under the banner of the Associated Loyalists. In February 1782, the Associated Loyalists launched a large raid that penetrated a dozen miles inland to Pleasant Valley, though the militia and state troops waged a formidable counterattack and recovered most of the plundered property. But an Associated Loyalist raid six weeks later succeeded in capturing the fort at Toms River and razing the village.

The Associated Loyalists were particularly angered by the conduct of Monmouth's Retaliators toward captured Loyalists (they documented the murder of thirteen Loyalists in Monmouth County). So they brought Captain Joshua Huddy—who had been captured while commanding the state troops at Toms River—back to Monmouth County and hanged him on the Navesink Highlands. They left his body swinging with a note pinned to his chest proclaiming that the hanging was an act of retaliation for the murder of the Loyalist Phillip White. White had been captured and killed two weeks earlier during a small Loyalist raid near Long Branch. Huddy's hangman, Moses, and the leader of the hanging party, Richard Lippincott, were both Loyalist refugees from the Monmouth County. The brazen murder of Huddy in retaliation for previous atrocities escalated into a diplomatic bonfire that involved George Washington, British commander in chief Sir Guy Carleton and leading figures in the American, British and French governments.

Civil warfare in Monmouth County declined toward the end of 1782. The British dry-docked the Associated Loyalists, and large raids were shut down. The last prolific Loyalist raider along the Raritan Bay shore, William Clark, was killed in July. Along the southern shore, the Pine Robber leader, Davenport, was killed, and his gang dispersed in June (though John Bacon remained active until finally meeting a bloody end in the spring of 1783). The Pine Robbers gangs were never fully defeated, but most melted back into civilian livelihoods. Violence ebbed. A handful of irregular clashes continued, particularly around Sandy Hook, but peace finally came to Monmouth County.

Even as hostilities cooled, David Forman and his allies continued taking provocative actions. Without legal authority, Forman led a band of men in the capture of a New England privateer and his two vessels (in fairness to Forman, it appears the privateer captain was illegally trading with the British). Forman also oversaw a gang of men who captured a small party of British sailors while on a routine trip to draw fresh water for their ship and severely beat them. The Retaliators stayed active and continued to meet into the summer of 1783. Finally, they, like the embittered Loyalists on the other side, ebbed in their activities.

POSTWAR

In Monmouth County, moderate Whigs, bolstered by former disaffecteds again participating in local government, won a string of elections. In 1785, election day coercion by the radicals resulted in their return to power. But the New Jersey legislature voided the election, and moderates won the state-ordered reelection. Several leading radicals—David Forman, Samuel Forman and Daniel Hendrickson—left the county; they crossed the Appalachians before the end of the 1780s, never to return.

Hundreds of Loyalists left Monmouth County because of the war. About 120 Loyalist estates—more than in any other New Jersey county—were confiscated. Over six hundred Monmouth Loyalists served in the New Jersey Volunteers. A large number of these men never returned home. Several dozen Monmouth County slaves sought protection behind British lines, and it is doubtful that they ever returned. The majority of Loyalists relocated to Canada, and their names are scattered across settler rolls throughout Canada's Maritime Provinces. Other Monmouthers settled on Staten Island and western Long Island during the war and stayed. A few went to England or the British Caribbean. In total, it can be reasonably estimated that about 10 percent of Monmouth County's population either died or went into exile because of the war.

The exodus of people was only one way the war changed Monmouth County. Before the war, only large landholders voted, and a handful of leading families monopolized important government offices. During the seven years of war, 358 Monmouthers held offices; an estimated one-third of these men did not even meet the property requirements necessary to vote before the war. Local politics during the war were raucous and often scandalous, but the war and independence brought true participatory democracy to Monmouth County. The county emerged from the crucible of civil warfare with credible leaders and competent governance.

The war opened up the Monmouth shore. Before the war, the shore mostly consisted of "unimproved" salt marsh. But salt making and privateering brought people, including well-capitalized investors, to the shore for the first time. Small ports like Toms River and Manasquan continued to grow after the privateers left. The increase in wealth and population in the shore townships is evidenced by the splitting in half of massive Shrewsbury Township into northern and southern townships in the 1790s and the creation of a new county—Ocean County—for the two lower townships of

Dover and Stafford in the 1800s. Prior to the war, these shore locales simply did not have the population to support their own political units.

The war also changed the families of Monmouth County, an estimated half of which suffered the loss of significant property or physical harm to a member during the war. With husbands deployed every second month on militia duty, women had to fill the void. Some women, such as Esther Frost, participated in the London trade and prospered. Frost grew her estate from three to eight livestock as her neighbors were plundered of theirs. Other women were victimized terribly during the war. Rebecca Dennis, widow of Captain John Dennis, was beaten with a gunstock by a Hessian soldier in June 1778 and then beaten by Pine Robbers plundering her home only a few months later. Still others behaved bravely by combating Loyalist raiders, as when Lucretia Emmons heroically assisted Joshua Huddy in holding off a Loyalist raiding party. A June 1780 militia return lists nineteen women along with the ninety-five men—probably women with the militia due to the danger of remaining at home. It is not a coincidence that three of the most poignant accounts of the American Revolution in Monmouth County were written by women: the sad veteran's pension narrative of Rhoda Sutphin, written as an old woman looking back at her and her husband's service; the letters of Amelia Dennis, recalling the abuse of her family by Pine Robbers; and the autobiography of Eliza Chadwick Roberts, recalling the capture of her father and murder of her uncle (both militia officers during the war). The seven years of civil and irregular warfare that consumed Monmouth County left few lives untouched.

2

"CONCEIVING OURSELVES IN A PRECARIOUS SITUATION"

The Extent of Civil Warfare in Monmouth County

The war years were hard on the Bennetts, a large extended family centered in Shrewsbury Township. As the Revolution began, the family split, with some joining Loyalist associations and others becoming solid Whigs. Some members of the Bennett family, such as Jeremiah Bennett, flipped back and forth.

Sometime shortly after the British landed on Sandy Hook and Staten Island, Jeremiah Bennett joined a secret Loyalist association at Shark River led by Samuel Wright. Bennett must have been among the more active members of the association, as he is one of only a few listed in two separate documents about Wright's group. The Loyalist association was discovered when Wright was captured by the Continental army upon his return from British lines. Bennett was among forty would-be Loyalists arrested and detained. He was interrogated by militia colonel Daniel Hendrickson on November 19, signed a loyalty oath to the new government and then was released. Many of his associates were shipped off to jail, presumably after refusing to sign the same oath Bennett signed. A few weeks later, the (Loyalist) New Jersey Volunteers under Colonel John Morris entered Shrewsbury Township at the start of the Loyalist ascendency. Bennett was friendly to the Loyalists during this time—at least until he was captured by the Whig militia. On December 18, he was sent to jail in Philadelphia.

Bennett was released from jail in early 1777 in exchange for signing another loyalty oath. He returned home, but because the militia companies from the shore neighborhoods were not mustering regularly, Bennett probably did not participate in any significant duty. In May 1778, when the New Jersey government enforced a draft from the county militias to fill the state's quota for the Continental army, Bennett was one of only a handful of Monmouthers drafted into service. As the draft was not random, Bennett was probably deliberately selected for the army as payback for his past loyalism. After serving in the Continental army, Bennett returned home and enlisted in the state troops. With money from military service (and likely some family assistance), Bennett was able to purchase a one-hundred-acre farm in 1779 and marry into a prominent Whig family (the Randolphs) in 1780. It appears Jeremiah Bennett's transformation into a prospering Whig was complete.

But the war was not over for Jeremiah Bennett. In 1781, he was plundered by Loyalist Pine Robbers. He signed a petition that December (the only petition he signed the entire war) calling for strong action against these Loyalist partisans. By 1784, Bennett was listed as only a "householder" in the tax rolls. Due to unpaid debts (perhaps exacerbated by plundering) or fearing for his safety, he had given up his farm. By war's end, he had lost the economic advantage he had temporarily gained.

———

Jeremiah Bennett is representative of hundreds of Monmouthers during the war—people with mixed feelings about independence who trimmed their sails and weathered the war. Leaders on both sides observed that the American countryside was filled with these so-called trimmers. This chapter looks at two important topics: 1) the range of political behavior in Monmouth County, from Revolutionaries on one side to Loyalists on the other, with trimmers and neutrals in the middle; and 2) the toll of the war on the people of Monmouth County.

By cataloging every adult man and woman to appear in Monmouth County's Revolutionary-era records, I was able to indentify about 5,500 men and 1,000 women. By cross-referencing these names with hundreds of lists—court records, petitions, military rolls, etc.—political loyalty can be assigned to about two-thirds of the men (3,596) but only a small number of women (118).

FIGURE 1: THE RANGE OF POLITICAL BEHAVIOR IN MONMOUTH COUNTY

SUPPORTERS OF INDEPENDENCE: WHIGS

Revolutionaries were the people who supported the cause of independence through voluntary and long-term military service in the Continental army or state troops, with all the sacrifices and dangers that were part of that service, or by holding an office linked to law enforcement (justice of the peace or judge of the courts) that exposed the officeholder to considerable danger. These people voluntarily risked their personal safety and property to support American independence. Based on surviving documentation, there were 627 Revolutionaries in Monmouth County. William Anderson of Middletown was one of them. In June 1776, he enlisted for six months in the Continental army's Flying Camp and fought at the Battle of Long Island. In October, he grew ill and was discharged home. In December, as Monmouth's Loyalists took control of the county, Anderson refused to sign a British loyalty oath. In January 1777, Anderson joined the re-formed Whig militia, where he served faithfully, even marching to Pennsylvania to fight at the Battle of Germantown. In June 1780, he enlisted for six months' continuous service in the state troops. There is no reason to think that Anderson was enriched by all this military service; he was listed as a single man in the 1784 Middletown tax ratables, showing that he was landless and poor at the war's conclusion.

Whigs supported the Revolutionary cause by serving in the militia, signing pro-war or pro-independence petitions or joining associations with a pro-Revolutionary purpose. These people were dutiful citizens to the new government but are distinguished from Revolutionaries because their actions did not involve voluntary activities expected to bring about great sacrifice. (Of course, militia service in Monmouth County was dangerous in its own right.) As militia service was widespread, 1,270 Monmouthers can be documented as Whigs. Zephanniah Morris was one such Whig. Morris was a small farmer (twenty acres, four livestock) from Middletown at the war's start. He did not volunteer for the Whig militia in 1776, but by 1777, when the militia was turning out regularly, he served in the militia's Dragoon

Company. He also gave testimony against a disaffected neighbor who refused to accept his Continental money to settle a debt and was elected the town constable in 1778. In 1779, Morris purchased a 176-acre confiscated Loyalist estate and moved to Shrewsbury Township to take possession of it. Soon after, he was captured on his new estate by Loyalist raiders and spent nearly a year as a prisoner before being exchanged. He was in a skirmish with Loyalist raiders later in the war. He is listed in the 1784 tax ratables as owning only a horse or cow, suggesting either great economic misfortune or the loss of livestock to Loyalist raiders.

OPPONENTS OF INDEPENDENCE: LOYALISTS

Loyalists were people who voluntarily supported the royal cause through serving in the British army's Provincial Corps, an irregular Loyalist partisan group, or by turning "refugee" and relocating to British-held New York. In any such case, these people voluntarily risked their lives and estates to oppose the Revolution. Monmouth County had 866 Loyalists based on surviving documents. One of those Loyalists was Thomas Woolley. Woolley was from a large Shrewsbury Township family that generally did not support the Revolution. In the fall of 1776, as British routs of the Continental army emboldened Loyalists, he joined a Loyalist association. Arrested in late November, Woolley was one of several dozen Monmouthers jailed in Pennsylvania. Woolley was released early in 1777 and returned home. In April 1777, he was arrested again and compelled to sign a loyalty oath to the new government as a condition of his release. But only a year later, he was serving as a private in the Loyalist New Jersey Volunteers at Sandy Hook, the staging ground for Loyalist incursions back into Monmouth County.

Disaffecteds were people who opposed the Revolution in a number of lesser ways, including committing misdemeanors with political undertones (that is, seditious words, unlawful assembly, illegal travel behind enemy lines), joining one of the Loyalist associations in 1776, refusing to support the militia or trading illegally with the British. These people demonstrated disaffection for the new government, but they expressed their opposition in only limited ways and did not risk their lives or estates for their political leanings. There were at least 674 disaffecteds in Monmouth County based on surviving documents, but because these people were covert or muted in expressing the views, this number surely understates the actual number of disaffecteds. William Parker, a yeoman Quaker from Shrewsbury Township, was one such disaffected. Early in the war, he cooperated with the new Whig government and was one of a set of Monmouthers to petition and receive a loan from the New Jersey government to start a saltworks on the New Jersey shore (to mitigate the salt shortage that followed the British naval blockade). But Parker refused to sell his cattle to the militia in April 1777 and was convicted of an unspecified misdemeanor (probably seditious speech or illegally trading with the British) in June 1778. Later in the war, he sheltered Loyalist raiders, and it appears that he evaded paying taxes in 1779 (taxes were not uniformly collected in Monmouth's more disaffected neighborhoods). Parker was probably plundered or abused at least once by vigilante Whigs; in 1782, he signed a petition to the New Jersey legislature claiming as much.

OTHERS

Trimmers were people who at various times took actions that, if examined individually, would place them alternatively in Whig or Loyalist camps. Due to the higher burden of proof needed to prove someone a trimmer, it is harder to document trimmers than any other political category. Based on surviving documents, there were at least 260 trimmers in Monmouth County (certainly many more). Patrick Bailey was one such trimmer. Bailey was from a Middletown family that included at least one Loyalist, Elias Bailey. Early in the war, Patrick Bailey joined the Loyalist New Jersey Volunteers before eventually deserting in January 1778. By 1780, he was back in Middletown behaving (at least publicly) as an enthusiastic Whig. In June, he voluntarily enlisted for six months' service in the state troops and also joined the vigilante Whigs of the Association for Retaliation that summer. But Bailey was probably still complicit in the rampant London trade that went on between disaffected Monmouthers and the British commissary at Sandy Hook, and he was charged with a misdemeanor (probably London trading) in January 1781.

Approximately 1,662 Monmouthers weathered the war as true neutrals or, due to inadequate documentation, cannot be placed in any other category.

MONMOUTH COUNTY'S WOMEN

Due to biases in the historical record, I was able to find politically relevant information on only 118 women. Still, there is enough documentation to offer revealing sketches of some of these women. Two interesting examples follow.

Deborah Williams was from a comfortable Quaker family from Shrewsbury Township, where she lived near her family's mill. Early in the war, her husband, John, went over to the British. Evidence suggests Deborah Williams was a Whig, even while living in a neighborhood where it was easy to express disaffection. She was one of nineteen women listed on a 1780 militia return compiled by Captain James Green, who was procuring rations for these "good" women as an expression of charity for their hardship (suggesting that the family mill was either destroyed or abandoned for fear of attack). Williams weathered the war, but her status in the 1784 rolls as a householder with only one cow indicates a considerable drop in wealth.

In contrast, Esther Frost is an example of a disaffected woman. She was a Middletown widow at the start of the war. Her disaffection was public, and she was charged with misdemeanors in both January and June 1778. In 1779, she married Marcus Headon, whose disaffection equaled hers, as shown by his three misdemeanor charges in 1781 and 1782. The fact that the Headons grew their livestock from three to eight head between 1778 and 1783 in a neighborhood where many Whigs were plundered of their livestock suggests that the Headons were friendly to or complicit with the London traders and Loyalist raiders who penetrated Middletown frequently in the latter half of the war.

WHIG MILITARY SERVICE

Men who wished to support independence could enlist in the Continental army or state troops or serve in the local militia. By New Jersey law, militia service was mandatory for able-bodied white adult males, but Monmouthers in much of the county faced no real penalty for skipping militia duty. Fines for skipping militia duty were issued inconsistently before 1780 and presumably only for repeated delinquency (it is not certain if fines were ever systematically collected). Therefore, faithful militia service was an expression of loyalty to the new government. A few professions were exempted from militia service: physicians, attorneys and salt makers. African Americans were also excluded from militia service but were allowed to serve in the Continental army. Devout Quakers banned themselves from bearing arms (for either side) due to their pacifist beliefs, though wartime events eventually caused at least thirty-six Monmouth Quakers to take up arms as Whigs and twenty-six to take up arms as Loyalists.

Thomas Curtis's wartime experience illustrates the difficult position faced by Quakers. Curtis was from a largely disaffected Shrewsbury family. For the first few years of the war, Curtis attempted to follow the path of neutrality, avoiding militia service and paying for a substitute when required. In April 1779, the Shrewsbury Friends censured him for paying for a substitute, as even this practice was viewed as tacitly supporting violence. After Curtis stopped paying for a substitute, he was twice fined for being delinquent from militia service. Arrested for militia delinquency, Curtis took a loyalty oath to the Whig government in order to win his release. This act again placed him in trouble with the Shrewsbury Friends (who opposed government oaths, holding that such solemn agreements were reserved for the religious sphere). When Curtis refused to renounce his oath and paid a fine for militia delinquency, he was disowned by the Shrewsbury Friends. But Curtis's banishment from the Shrewsbury Friends did not improve his status with the Whigs. He was arrested twice more and charged with unspecified misdemeanors in 1781 and 1782, probably seditious speech against the Whig government or participating in the London trade.

Monmouth County had three militia regiments. The First Regiment (ten companies) was drawn from Middletown and Freehold Townships, the Second (eight companies) was drawn from Shrewsbury Township and the Third (eight companies) was drawn from Upper Freehold, Dover and Stafford Townships. Of the three, only the First Regiment mustered reliably throughout the war. The First Regiment marched to Pennsylvania to support the Continental army at the Battle of Germantown and attached itself to the New Jersey Militia in the days leading up to the Battle of Monmouth in June 1778. In the second half of the war, it turned out fairly reliably to battle Loyalist raiding parties. The Second Regiment was dysfunctional through most of the war. Its first colonel, Samuel Breese, resigned in frustration, and its second, Daniel Hendrickson, spent long stretches of time captured and confined in New York or inland in Upper Freehold for his own safety. Hendrickson and most of the regiment's senior officers were captured in a June 1779 raid against Tinton Falls. It appears that only the company from the inland village of Colts Neck, commanded by Captain

James Green, mustered regularly, though Captains Daniel Hampton and Stephen Fleming attempted to enforce turnout starting in 1780. The Third Regiment was the most opportunistic; the three companies from the lower shore townships of Dover and Stafford attacked British/Loyalist shipping with great enthusiasm. But these same companies generally turned a blind eye to the London trader and Pine Robber gangs that operated in their midst; in many cases, the militiamen were themselves London traders. The Upper Freehold militia companies increased in regularity over the course of the war, but their inland location limited their actual service. Over twelve hundred Monmouthers are documented as serving at least one militia tour.

At least 316 Monmouth Whigs performed extended military service beyond the militia. A company of Monmouthers first mustered into the Continental army in 1775 under Captain Elias Longstreet, but the first large-scale mobilization was in the spring of 1776, when four companies were raised for six months' service under Colonel David Forman. Forman was authorized to raise an additional regiment for the Continental army in January 1777, but recruiting went poorly, and it appears the total strength of that body never went much above 100 men. After a string of controversies, this unit was merged into New Jersey's Continental Line in 1778. In addition, companies of New Jersey State Troops were raised from the county in every year of the war except 1778, reaching peak strength (over 200 strong) in 1780. Of the 316 Monmouth Whigs who performed long-term duty outside the militia, 240 can be traced to a township of residence. Of these men, over 40 percent (102 of the 240) lived in Freehold Township, which had under 20 percent of the county's entire population. This suggests a great unevenness within the county with respect to zealousness for the Whig cause.

John Bennett (not a close relative of Jeremiah Bennett) is one Whig with a long and varied military service. In 1775, he enlisted in the first company of Monmouthers to join the Continental army, and his company took part in the ill-fated Canadian campaign that winter. He likely stayed in the Continental army after his one-year enlistment expired because he does not show up again in Monmouth County records until 1779, when he returned home and married Sarah Logan, suggesting he had accumulated some money during his time away from home. In December 1779, his militia detachment seized the beached British brig *Britannia*. In early 1780, he was serving in the Monmouth militia's light horse company, where he likely served until enlisting for six months' service in the state troops in June 1782. In 1783, he joined an association committed to opposing the return of Loyalists at the war's conclusion.

LOYALIST MILITARY SERVICE

Those who wished to oppose the Revolution had many options in a county like Monmouth. Loyalists could join the New Jersey Volunteers, and 605 Monmouthers did, or they could join other units in the British military. A few dozen served in other Loyalist units such as Roger's Rangers, the West Jersey Volunteers and the Royal Navy. Other Loyalists served the royal cause in other ways, including a Loyalist militia commanded by Colonel George Taylor (discussed in the next chapter) and irregular groups like the Associated Loyalists and the ungoverned gangs of Pine Robbers and cowboys who plundered along the Atlantic shore and Raritan Bay shore, respectively.

On July 2, 1776, even before the signing of the Declaration of Independence, sixty Monmouth Loyalists from the shore townships, led by John Morris, marched to Sandy Hook and joined the British army. Along with a similar group from Freehold and Upper Freehold Townships led by Elisha Lawrence, these men became the core of the New Jersey Volunteers, the largest Loyalist corps raised in the Thirteen Colonies. Over six hundred Monmouthers eventually served in the New Jersey Volunteers (about 30 percent of all men to serve in the New Jersey Volunteers and more than 10 percent of the county's adult male population).

In September 1777, the New Jersey Volunteers were surprised by a large Continental raiding party and routed in their camp on Staten Island. Lieutenant Colonel Elisha Lawrence and many others were captured. After this, it appears the New Jersey Volunteers withered in size and effectiveness. Dozens deserted in 1777 and 1778 and reappear in Monmouth County's tax rolls by the war's end. However, most of these deserters remained disaffected on some level throughout the war. Based on surviving documentation, at least twenty-seven (and probably many more) New Jersey Volunteer deserters became Loyalist partisans later in the war, including the infamous Pine Robber Jacob Fagan and some of his associates. Many others integrated back into disaffected shore communities, where they skipped militia service, evaded taxes and participated in the London trade.

William Reynolds Sr. was one Monmouther who started the war in the New Jersey Volunteers and concluded the war as a Loyalist irregular. Reynolds was living modestly as a householder in Upper Freehold Township when he enlisted in the New Jersey Volunteers on December 16, 1776, at the height of the Loyalist ascendancy in Monmouth County. But he served only a short time, deserting on February 5, 1777. (His son, William Jr., stayed in the New Jersey Volunteers and died in service soon after.) Reynolds probably tried to live as a neutral during the middle years of the war, resettling in Upper Freehold. But by 1780, he was residing in Middletown, where he became involved in London trading, for which he was convicted. By 1782, Reynolds was a Loyalist again, participating in irregular raiding activity that earned him an indictment for horse stealing in the county courts. By war's end, he was among the Loyalist boatmen at Sandy Hook, alternately raiding Whig farmsteads, London trading and fishing for a living.

It is difficult to trace Loyalist service through the entire war. Surviving muster rolls for the New Jersey Volunteers are generally intact through 1777 but fall off badly by the middle years of the war, and only a few haphazardly exist beyond 1779. The consolidation of the New Jersey Volunteers from six regiments to three by war's end indicates great attrition (primarily due to desertion, expiration of enlistment and death from sickness). While a few dozen Monmouthers went from the New Jersey Volunteers to other Loyalist pursuits, such as other Loyalist corps, the British navy or the Associated Loyalists, it is impossible to trace most Monmouth Loyalists over the course of the war.

A NOTE ON TRIMMERS

Finally, at least 207 Monmouthers (probably many more) served in Loyalist units or associations at one point during the war, only to serve in the Whig military at other times. Most of these trimmers started the war in Loyalist associations and the New Jersey Volunteers and then abandoned the Loyalist cause when the British retreated across New Jersey and the Loyalist ascendancy collapsed in January 1777. They were serving in the Whig county militia or state troops by war's end. John North was one Loyalist who became an ardent Whig. North was from a modest Shrewsbury family that produced Whigs and Loyalists during the war. In late 1776, North joined Samuel Wright's Loyalist association. When Wright was exposed, North joined the New Jersey Volunteers but did not serve more than a few weeks. North was captured in January 1777 and jailed in Philadelphia. In March 1777, he petitioned for clemency and was released on the condition that he enlist in the Continental army, which he joined in May. By the later years of the war, North was home in Shrewsbury Township, where he transformed himself into a zealous Whig. In January 1782, he enlisted in the state troops; in March, he was in a party of three men who took possession of the captured Loyalist Phillip White and participated in White's murder. In December 1782, North was indicted for riot, though the specifics of the charge are not known.

THE TOLL OF LOCAL WARFARE

The low casualty rates from the Revolution's major battles (rarely more than a few hundred battlefield deaths) have led many to conclude that the American Revolution was not a particularly bloody conflict. But because the American Revolution was also a civil war, an understanding of the war's full destruction and human toll needs a wider focus. Casualties and captures from skirmishes between small bodies of militia and irregular groups, the destruction of private property, vigilantism and political violence and punishments for political crimes are all part of civil war. With this broader focus, it becomes clear that the American Revolution was quite destructive in Monmouth County. In total, 1,081 individuals can be documented as suffering: 143 were killed, 77 wounded, 332 captured and confined, 372 plundered of property and 379 legally punished. As high as these numbers are, as will be discussed, the real toll of war was certainly much higher (perhaps 50 percent higher based on my previous research) due to large gaps in the historical record.

Loyalists suffered proportionately more than Whigs. While living under the Whig government, a substantial number of disaffected Monmouthers (190 to be exact) suffered various legal punishments, generally fines and detention. In addition, 127 Monmouth Loyalists lost their estates through a formal confiscation process.

Samuel Layton, a small Shrewsbury landholder at the start of the war, can be used to illustrate Loyalist suffering. Layton supported the Loyalist insurrections of late 1776, and on January 1, 1777, as Whigs were regaining control of the county, Layton fled behind British lines. By August 1777, he was serving in the New Jersey Volunteers and was captured on Staten Island by a party of Continentals. He was confined as a prisoner for at least four months. In June 1778, the New Jersey government inventoried his estate for forfeiture; in May 1779, it was sold at public auction.

While Loyalists suffered proportionately more often due to legal punishment and property confiscation, Whigs suffered capture far more often than

Loyalists (128 to 72). The bulk of these Whig captures were militiamen living near enemy lines and state troops. Documentation on what happened to these Whigs during confinement is frustratingly sketchy, but it is known that large numbers were incarcerated on the dismal prison ships in New York Harbor, including the dreaded prison ship *Jersey*, where the death toll was considerable. More than a dozen Monmouth Whigs, including James Johnson of Shrewsbury, were captured more than once during the war.

Johnson was a small farmer from Shrewsbury who mustered in the militia at the start of the war (June 1776). It appears he served faithfully despite residing in an area where he probably faced no penalty for skipping service. In June 1780, Johnson was captured while part of a militia guard that was overpowered by a party of mostly African American Loyalist raiders; he was jailed for several months. Finally exchanged, Johnson enlisted in the state troops in January 1782. He was serving at Toms River in March 1782 when he was wounded and captured—and jailed again. At war's end, his estate had suffered (decreasing from four livestock in 1779 to one in 1784), and he joined an association of zealous Whigs committed to opposing the reintegration of Loyalists. He endured months on the dismal British prisoner ships and reaped no benefits from his long service and time in confinement.

LEADERSHIP AND SUFFERING

Whether Whig or Loyalist, leaders faced great risk. One-third of Whig leaders suffered during the war, and two-thirds of Loyalist leaders suffered. For both Whig and Loyalist leaders, about half of the instances of suffering involved bodily harm (death, capture or wounding). High-profile Whig leaders were the targets of raids, as when Loyalist raids were launched to capture Reverend Charles McKnight in 1777 or Lieutenant Colonel John Smock in 1780. Other Whig leaders like Lieutenant Colonel Thomas Seabrook and Colonel Daniel Hendrickson moved inland for safety (though Seabrook's rented farm in Manalapan was ruined during the fighting at the Battle of Monmouth, and Hendrickson was captured on his return to Tinton Falls in 1779). A few Whig leaders were killed in combat, such as Lieutenant Jeremiah Chadwick in 1779, Congressman Nathaniel Scudder in 1781 and Major John Cook in 1782. Loyalist leaders lost their estates and faced violence from retribution-minded Whigs. For example, Joseph Allen, a surveyor, and Dr. James Boggs both fled their homes after narrow escapes from Whig mobs, and other Loyalist leaders were captured while serving in the New Jersey Volunteers, such as Lieutenant Colonel Elisha Lawrence and Major Thomas Leonard.

Joshua Studson's rise and fall illustrates the increased risks that came with being a leader. Studson was a resident of Toms River, the lone Whig village on the disaffected Monmouth shoreline. Despite his modest estate (twenty-three acres, one cow) and no evidence of prominence before the war, Studson distinguished himself as a militia sergeant and the master of a privateer whaleboat (see text box below). In May 1778, Studson captured a British vessel near Sandy Hook. Two years later, Studson was one of only a handful of Dover Township Whigs to join the vigilante Whig group the Retaliators. His zeal for the Whig cause was rewarded in 1780, when he was elected militia lieutenant, appointed a recruiter for the state troops and elected surveyor of the highways for Dover Township. Despite holding three offices concurrently, Studson continued to be an active privateer and succeeded in capturing two more prizes in 1780. But Studson's rise was abruptly ended on December 20, 1780. He was shot and killed while standing up and giving orders in a militia boat as it pursued a party of Loyalist irregulars near Toms River. Interestingly, in March 1782, when the Associated Loyalists razed Toms River, the house of widow Studson was one of only two buildings in the village that was spared the torch.

WHALEBOAT PRIVATEERS

Monmouth County privateers were active as early as 1776 and captured dozens of British or Loyalist vessels over the course of the war. Lacking deep-water ports, most local privateers used whaleboats. Whaleboats were large rowboats that were pointed on both ends and carried as many as sixteen men. They were often fitted out with small turreted cannons (called swivel guns) on one or both ends. Oars were often wrapped with cloth or leather strips to make them quieter. Whaleboat privateers had their greatest success when surprising and boarding larger vessels at night. Whigs also used these boats when conducting nocturnal raids against Sandy Hook, Staten Island and Brooklyn. Loyalist irregulars also used whaleboats against Whigs.

At least for Whigs, holding a militia commission was more dangerous than holding a civilian leadership position (which helps explain why so many companies in the Monmouth militia were dysfunctional). In total, eighty-seven acts of suffering befell the 187 Monmouthers who held commissions in the Monmouth militia. About half of these were captures, an outcome from battle, raids or premeditated kidnappings called "man-stealing." Not surprisingly, militia officers from the two townships closest to the British base at Sandy Hook (Shrewsbury and Middletown) suffered the most (over 40 percent suffered bodily harm), while Upper Freehold's militia officers, shielded by an inland location that made raids on their homes impossible, were by far the safest (only 6 percent suffered bodily harm).

CONCLUSION

Revolutionary Monmouth County split into roughly equal blocs of Whigs and Loyalists, with a large trimmer and neutral center vacillating in between. In a county with fewer than 6,000 adult males, 605 risked their lives and property to enlist in the Loyalist New Jersey Volunteers and other British military units; nearly as many risked their lives in the Continental army and the New Jersey State Troops. Over 1,200 Whigs served in the militia, and several hundred disaffecteds joined Loyalist associations and partisan groups. In total, it can be conservatively estimated that two-thirds of Monmouth's male population took up arms during the war—a notable figure in a county with a large number of (pacifist) Quakers and several weakly governed areas in which people could not be effectively forced into military service.

The war was hard on the people of Monmouth County. Over 20 percent of adult men—almost eleven hundred people—suffered a harmful event, and three hundred of these men suffered more than one. About half of these events involved bodily harm (capture, death or wounding), and it can be reasonably estimated that these numbers undercount the real number of violent harmful events by about 50 percent. Even serving in the militia, the most passive form of military service, carried considerable risk. Militiamen engaged in dozens of battles and skirmishes during the war, and active militiamen were the focus of robberies and kidnappings. All of these numbers are best understood when placed in the perspective of their effect on the entire family. Based on typical family size and the likely distribution of harmful events across families, it can be reasonably estimated that about half of Monmouth County's families suffered a harmful event during the war.

In May 1777, the residents of Dover Township anticipated the civil warfare that would soon overtake them and damage so many of their lives. In a petition to the New Jersey legislature, they noted that "the militia are not very numerous and hard to collect on any occasion, and [we are] conceiving ourselves in a precarious situation." They requested a detachment of Continental soldiers to help the small local militia protect the shore. The petition went unanswered.

This was one of several petitions written by Monmouth Whigs praying for greater protection. But, as noted, Loyalists and disaffecteds living along the military frontier were at least as vulnerable. The next chapter provides a case study in the ways war adversely impacted the lives of two Loyalists—one who attempted to weather the war peacefully at home and the other who became an active opponent of the Revolution.

This chapter draws on research first presented in the essay "An Evenly Balanced County," published in the *Journal of Military History in January 2009.*

3

"I Am as Innocent as an Unborn Child"

The Loyalism of Edward and George Taylor

O f all Monmouth County's churches, none split as acrimoniously as the county's Baptists. As the war began, the Baptist rolls included some of the county's leading Whig families (Motts, Wallings and Carharts) but also some of its leading disaffected families (Taylors, Grovers and Baileys). In early 1777, Monmouth's Baptists split over whether to tolerate disaffected members within their meeting and temporarily stopped assembling. The deacon of the Upper Freehold Baptist meeting, Thomas Farr, commented in March, "No meeting—these are troublesome times indeed."

Soon after, the Middletown Baptists took action. They voted to "joyn [*sic*] with the Free States of America…against our cruel enemies" and called for "a purging time" within their ranks. At the same meeting, Elias Bailey and David Burdge, two Middletown Loyalists living in New York, were formally excommunicated. Two weeks later, the meeting discussed a motion to disbar other Loyalist members, including John Taylor and William Grover (Taylor and Grover had played prominent roles in the Loyalist ascendancy a few months earlier).

John Taylor's brother, Edward Taylor, was known to be disaffected from the new government, but his disloyalty was more muted than his brother's outright loyalism. The meeting appointed James Crawford and Richard Mott to meet with Edward Taylor and "warn him to forebear talking so much against the present state, and in behalf of the Enemy." Though it censured Edward Taylor, the Baptist meeting did not expel him. And on

May 24, Edward Taylor cast the only dissenting vote in the congregation's decision to disbar his brother. It appears Edward Taylor stopped attending the Baptist meeting afterward and suffered many insults—great and small—from his former co-congregants after that.

Four years later, a fifteen-hundred-man Loyalist and British raiding party, guided by Monmouth Loyalists who fled to the British in New York, came through Middletown. The Baptist meetinghouse was razed. The odds are good that Edward's revenge-minded son, George Taylor, guided the raiding party that razed the church.

Historians have struggled to explain the Loyalist experience in the American Revolution because the term is so broad. It can be applied to virtually anyone from aristocratic royal appointees to opportunistic locals whose loyalism was based only on small-town or clan rivalry. And some Loyalists came to their loyalism later than others. Many Americans who led anti-British dissent in the colonies in 1774–75 became Loyalists afterward, when they perceived Whigs as abusing their power or when the inflationary new currencies depreciated the value of their estates. In Monmouth County and elsewhere throughout the Middle Colonies, there were many so-called Whig-Loyalists, people who vigorously protested British policy and abuses of power but turned Loyalist before or during the string of British triumphs around New York City (fall 1776). Whig-Loyalists included people like John Dickinson of Pennsylvania, whose writings inspired the dissent that led to the First Continental Congress and the intercolonial boycott of British goods before he ultimately decided that revolution against the British Empire was a bridge too far.

This chapter focuses on a segment of Monmouth County's prewar leaders who went the same route as Dickinson. In particular, it traces Edward and George Taylor, who, because of excellent surviving documentation, are ideal case studies for this understudied segment of colonial leadership: people who led anti-British dissent but turned Loyalist when dissent turned into rebellion. The American Revolution along the military frontier was particularly hard on these people.

THE TAYLORS OF MIDDLETOWN

In the years leading up to the Revolution, the Taylors of Middletown were among the most prominent and politically active families in Monmouth County. The family's two patriarchs, brothers Edward and John, were wealthy farmer-merchants with significant investments and commercial ties to New York City. Their importance is proven by the fact that they owned the two most notable homes in Middletown, Edward residing in Marlpit Hall on King's Highway and John residing in Middletown's largest home, jealously nicknamed "Taylor's Folly." In addition to holding local offices, Edward Taylor served as one of Monmouth County's two popularly elected delegates in the New Jersey Assembly. John Taylor spent several years in the 1760s as Monmouth County's high sheriff. Edward and John Taylor also had prominent sons. George Taylor, son of Edward, was a wealthy farmer with holdings in both Middletown and Shrewsbury Townships; he also served as Middletown's town clerk and as colonel of the county militia.

FIGURE 2: THE TAYLOR FAMILY

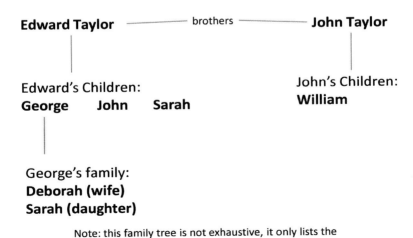

The Taylor Family of Middletown

Note: this family tree is not exhaustive, it only lists the individuals discussed in this chapter.

John Taylor's oldest son, William, was a well-connected lawyer in Freehold (the county seat), who served as the county's court solicitor, a patronage position in the royal government. At the start of the pre-Revolutionary agitation, Edward and George Taylor held elected offices, as assemblyman and colonel of the county militia; John and William Taylor held patronage positions in the royal government, as judge of the court of general sessions and court solicitor.

THE POLITICAL CAREER OF EDWARD TAYLOR

In the years prior to the American Revolution, no Monmouth County resident was as active or prominent in local politics as Edward Taylor. From 1769 through its final session, Edward Taylor served as one of Monmouth County's two delegates in New Jersey's Provincial Assembly. Taylor's long tenure in the assembly demonstrates that he was respected by the people of Monmouth County (at least the minority of men wealthy enough to vote), who reelected him annually. Edward Taylor's political activities in the years immediately preceding the American Revolution demonstrate his political leadership and Whig politics. In April 1774, Taylor chaired the first countywide meeting held in Monmouth County for the purpose of resisting British policies. At the meeting, the committeemen elected delegates to represent the county at the upcoming province-wide convention. The meeting selected seven delegates, including Edward Taylor and his brother, John. The convention met at New Brunswick in May. Two of its more significant accomplishments were: 1) the establishment of a committee of correspondence to communicate with Whigs in other provinces and coordinate a boycott of British goods and 2) the election of a delegation to attend the First Continental Congress. As the senior member from one of New Jersey's more important counties, Edward Taylor probably played a major role at the convention.

On July 19, 1774, leading citizens from four of Monmouth County's six townships met at Freehold (Shrewsbury and Stafford Townships did not attend) for the purpose of establishing a county committee of correspondence. Edward Taylor chaired the meeting. The meeting established a countywide committee of correspondence and instructed each of the townships to do the same. It also composed a charter, defining its Whig principles. The committee stated its clear opposition to the policies of the British government, calling it:

altogether unprecedented and unconstitutional, utterly inconsistent with the Principles of the Magna Carta, subversive to the Rights of Free-born Englishmen and tending directly to the dissolution and destruction of the British Empire.

It also stated its support for the citizens of Massachusetts (suffering under the Boston Port Bill) and pledged to continue the boycott of British goods "until such oppressive acts be repealed and the Liberties of America be restored."

Yet the charter of the Monmouth County committee was far from a pro-independence document. Despite their protests, the Monmouth Whigs affirmed their loyalty to King George, declaring that they wished to:

transmit testimony of their loyalty to his Britannic Majesty, that they do highly esteem and prize the happiness of being governed by so Excellent a system of Laws as that of Great Britain, doubtless the best in the Universe.

Furthermore, the committee denounced as dangerous "that Spirit of Independence...which has been of late, held up to the attention of the Nation." As chairman, the charter of the Monmouth County committee was no doubt the embodiment of Edward Taylor's political views. On the one hand, it was a vigorous statement of protest against oppressive British policies. Yet it was also an emphatic statement of loyalty to the British king and culture. In 1774, there was no reason to think these two positions were irreconcilable.

Edward Taylor was busy through the fall and winter of 1774–75. He attended the New Jersey Assembly, where he was part of a considerable Whig bloc. He was also one of the members of the assembly who went to observe the First Continental Congress and report on its progress. Meanwhile, Edward Taylor continued to be active in local Whig committees, serving on the Monmouth County Committee of Correspondence and the newly formed Middletown Township Committee. One of the main activities of these committees that winter was raising food for the city of Boston. By December 1774, the Monmouth County committees raised "eleven hundred and forty bushels of rye, and fifty barrels of rye meal, for the suffering poor of that town." Edward Taylor led the effort to raise these foodstuffs, and it was Taylor who wrote the letter accompanying their shipment. Taylor wrote to a colleague that he "wrote them [the people of Boston] not to give up, and if they should want a further supply of bread, to let us know." Six weeks later, when a thank-you note arrived from Boston, it was sent to Edward Taylor.

News of the Battles of Lexington and Concord prompted another province-wide convention. Again, Edward Taylor attended as one of Monmouth's representatives. The convention agreed that New Jersey needed a governing body outside of royal influence and called for a Provincial Congress to meet at Trenton on May 23, 1775. The Provincial Congress of New Jersey would hold five sessions over the next year, and Edward Taylor was the only Monmouther selected to attend every session. By early 1776, the Provincial Congress was emerging as the de facto government of New Jersey. It passed laws to raise revenues, organized a new militia, broadened the electorate and sent a delegation to the Second Continental Congress. Yet as the Provincial Congress was evolving into a real government, Edward Taylor was evolving from Whig to Loyalist.

By 1776, protests and boycotts were giving way to violence and the establishment of a new government. This proved too radical a transition for Edward Taylor. Edward Taylor's first resistance to the Whig tide was on February 16, 1776, when the New Jersey Provincial Congress voted to lower suffrage requirements. The new law more than doubled the size of the electorate (of course, women and African Americans still could not vote). Though the measure passed, Edward Taylor, chairing the Monmouth delegation, voted against it. Also sometime in early 1776, the Middletown Township Committee passed a resolution that denounced "the avowed designs of the Ministry of Great Britain to raise revenue in America" and pledged to "support and carry into execution whatever measures may be recommended by the Provincial or Continental Congress." Apparently fearing the unconditional vote of confidence given to the Continental Congress, Taylor was one of two committee members to oppose the measure, signing it with the words "nay & nil" next to his name. Further, Taylor continued in his loyalty to the old New Jersey Assembly. He was one of many members of the Provincial Congress who simultaneously served in the recessed assembly, but he was one of only two members of the Provincial Congress not to resign from the assembly when Royal Governor William Franklin threatened to call the assembly into session during a session of the Provincial Congress (a move calculated to make individuals serving in both bodies choose between one or the other).

Soon, Edward Taylor was forced to decide between Whiggery and loyalism. On June 7, 1776, Governor Franklin threw down the gauntlet. He called for the Provincial Congress at Trenton to disband in a week's time and for the assembly to reconvene at Perth Amboy on June 20. On June 14, the Provincial Congress, by a wide majority, voted to ignore the governor's edict, and on June 17, it voted to arrest Governor Franklin. Edward Taylor opposed these measures. On June 21, Taylor was one of only three delegates to vote against a law empowering militia officers to arrest citizens for public displays against the new New Jersey government. What probably happened next is that Taylor left the Provincial Congress in protest of the rebellious measures. On June 26, the New Jersey Provincial Congress ordered Colonel Abraham Teneyck to apprehend twenty-six prominent New Jersey citizens whose loyalty to the new regime was in doubt and "keep them under a strong guard, [then] deliver them to the Common Gaol at Trenton." Edward Taylor was on the list; the transition from Whig to Loyalist was complete.

Exactly what Edward Taylor did to warrant arrest is unclear. According to Colonel Teneyck's orders, Taylor was only to be detained until his appearance before the Provincial Congress could be arranged. Taylor's status among his former peers and the lenient policies of the Provincial Congress toward prominent Loyalists probably meant a light punishment for Taylor. But this first punishment did not curb Edward Taylor's growing disaffection. In the following months, he refused to conduct business in Continental currency and lampooned the Continental Congress's fiscal policy, claiming that it "has two people employed from morning to night to print [worthless] Continental money." Edward Taylor also took two loyalty oaths to the British during the Loyalist insurrection of December 1776. He probably supported the short-lived Loyalist government in Monmouth County for which his brother, John, served as high commissioner. By the start of 1777, Edward Taylor had sided with the Loyalists, though his actions never went so far as to openly serve the British war effort.

The Military Service of George Taylor

While Edward Taylor was Monmouth County's leading political figure in the months leading up to the Revolution, his oldest son, George, was the county's leading military figure. When forty-eight Monmouthers from Middletown assembled in July 1775 to create a new militia loyal to the Provincial Congress, George Taylor was elected its first captain. In September 1775, at another public meeting to organize a Whig county militia, George Taylor was elected the first colonel.

George Taylor's election by his men to the highest rank in the county militia proves his high status and popularity before the war. It also suggests that he was viewed as a moderate, acceptable to independence-minded radicals in Freehold and shore residents who were skeptical of the Provincial Congress and the Whig movement. (In Shrewsbury, the largest township in the county, residents repeatedly refused to honor the boycott on British goods or even establish a township committee. Shrewsbury's refusal to form a committee resulted in the township being temporarily "separated" from the rest of the county by the Monmouth County committee.) George Taylor probably represented a perfect compromise between the Freehold radicals and the Shrewsbury disaffected, a man whom both sides could believe was with them. Two February 1776 petitions to the Provincial Congress urged the Provincial Congress to exempt George Taylor from the militia law and let him hold the ranks of colonel for the entire county and company captain for his neighborhood simultaneously. This suggests that George Taylor may have been the only man acceptable across the broad political spectrum in Monmouth County.

In March 1776, the Provincial Congress of New Jersey and the New York Convention of Delegates agreed on a joint mission to disable the lighthouse at Sandy Hook to prevent its use by the British navy. It was agreed that Major William Malcolm of New York, with a party of his men, would sail to New Jersey and then proceed alongside a New Jersey party to the lighthouse. Once at the lighthouse, orders were explicit:

> *You will endeavour* [sic] *to take the glass out of the lantern, and save it if possible; but if you find it impracticable, you will break all the glass. You will endeavour* [sic] *to pump oil out of the cisterns into casks and bring it off; but if you should be obstructed in your tasks by the Enemy, you will pump it on the ground. In short, you will use your best discretion to render the light-house entirely useless.*

George Taylor led the New Jersey party in this expedition. On March 8, the Taylor-Malcolm expedition went to the lighthouse, broke the lantern and carried off a number of items essential to its operation. On March 8, Malcolm reported back to the New York Convention, noting:

> *Having broken out the glass of the lantern, and delivered them over, the 8th inst., to Col. George Taylor of Middletown, New Jersey, eight copper lamps, two tackle falls and blocks, and three casks and one half a cask of oil.*

George Taylor kept the lighthouse items under his care, presumably storing them on his own premises. Despite removing the lighthouse items, the Taylor-Malcolm mission was not successful. A British naval squadron landed at the unguarded Sandy Hook Lighthouse in April 1776, and the lighthouse was operational again by early June, in time to light the way for the British fleet that arrived at the end of the month.

George Taylor was changed by the British arrival at Sandy Hook in June 1776 and his father's growing disaffection. Throughout June and July 1776, George Taylor commanded the Monmouth County militia opposite the British camp on Sandy Hook; his record as a military commander in this period is poor. On June 21, 1776, a Continental army detachment under Lieutenant Colonel Benjamin Tupper unsuccessfully attacked the Sandy Hook Lighthouse. In his letter to George Washington describing the attack, Tupper complained about Taylor's men offering no help, writing, "I received no assistance from the Jersies, tho' it was earnestly requested." (See chapter 5 for more on Tupper's campaign against Sandy Hook.) The same day, George Taylor was the only senior officer in the Monmouth militia to sign a petition to the New Jersey Provincial Congress arguing against independence and war with Great Britain. The petition stated:

> We trust, Gentlemen, that you will have the Honour, the interest and the safety and welfare of your native Country too much at heart to subject this once flourishing Province to the reproachful and calamitous consequences of an avowed separation...We are convinced that settlements of Separation and Independence must not only be impolitic, but may be of the most dangerous and destructive Consequences.

Like his father, George Taylor's views were becoming irreconcilable with the actions of New Jersey's leading Whigs.

Yet while this is clear in retrospect, it was not so apparent in June 1776, and the government of New Jersey continued relying on George Taylor throughout the summer. On June 26, the Provincial Congress appointed George Taylor as commissary for the company of state troops, under Captain Joseph Stillwell, arriving at the Navesink Highlands. This company of recruits and the Monmouth militia under George Taylor were all that stood between thousands of arriving British soldiers and the interior of New Jersey.

On June 29, 1776, George Taylor informed the Provincial Congress that a flotilla of British warships, the first wave of the anticipated British invasion, was at Sandy Hook. The Provincial Congress still trusted Taylor totally, relying on him as their principal source of intelligence at this critical time. But the appearance of the British fleet at the Hook shook Taylor's confidence in the new government even further. That same day, George Taylor sent a desperate plea to the Provincial Congress, praying for more troops. He predicted that "the Party of Men and light Horse at Sandy Hook, I have no doubt, will pay us a visit as soon as convenient to them. Our guard is very weak and not sufficient to make any stand." Just a few days later, Taylor protested to the Provincial Congress in response to a plan to split his command in half and march half the men off to New York to support the Continental army. John Covenhoven of Freehold, also vice-president of the Provincial Congress, summarized the letter. He noted:

> *We also received a letter from Colo. Taylor of Monmouth County, informing us that the county being so exposed to the Enemy without & Tories among them besides, that he apprehends that the Militia will not be possible to march to New-York & leave their wives and Children to fall Prey to the Enemy or to be murdered by the Tories, who are embodying themselves in a considerable camp in the cedar Swamps.*

It is unlikely that Covenhoven or anyone else doubted George Taylor's loyalty. While it is probable that George Taylor was disaffected by June 1776, it was the events of July that ultimately drove him into actively opposing the Whig movement. On July 2, the New Jersey Provincial Congress (now calling itself the Convention of New Jersey) ratified a new constitution, creating a government totally independent from British authority. Just two weeks earlier, George Taylor signed a petition arguing against any such move. In the next week came the Declaration of Independence and the British invasion of Staten Island, making war with the British inevitable. This must have been especially unnerving for George Taylor, who from his post on the Navesink Highlands witnessed the unopposed landing of the British. Then, on July 18, the New Jersey legislature converted George Taylor's militia regiment into state troops and ordered him to lead them off to New York to join the Continental army in its upcoming showdown with the British army.

However, George Taylor's men never made it beyond Perth Amboy, and then they returned to Monmouth County. George Taylor likely played a role in this quasi mutiny; he was probably irritated by the government's inability to promptly reimburse him for the soldiers' wages paid out of his own pocket while acting as commissary officer. Sometime before July 26, George Taylor left the state troops and returned home. He may have resigned from the state troops, but he still retained his position as senior colonel of the county militia.

Back home in largely disaffected eastern Monmouth County, it was not long before George Taylor began working against the Continental cause. On July 26, he, without authority to do so, issued passes to three Shrewsbury Loyalists—Joseph Wardell, John Corlies and George Allen—to visit the British army on Staten Island in an attempt to retrieve three runaway slaves. This incident drew the attention of the New York Convention of Delegates, which wrote to the Shrewsbury committee for an explanation. The New Yorkers accused Taylor of improperly issuing the passes, writing of the Loyalists, "They went under Colonel Taylor's permission." George Taylor was chastised by Josiah Holmes of the Shrewsbury Committee of Observation, but the rebuke did not curb Taylor's disaffection. By September, George Taylor was secretly "a friend" of Samuel Wright, a Shrewsbury Loyalist recruiting men for the New Jersey Volunteers. Taylor supported Wright's group with provisions. A few weeks later, George Taylor "offered every assistance" to Daniel Van Mater, a Middletown Loyalist who was secretly gathering horses and wagons for the British army.

Nevertheless, George Taylor continued to be trusted by the New Jersey government, even as he secretly worked against it. On August 21, 1776, the New Jersey legislature voted to reimburse him £160 for the costs he incurred while serving as commissary officer—evidence of his continued good standing. And on October 17, George Taylor was ordered to take custody of the Boston-owned merchant ship *Betsy*, which had been beached on the Shrewsbury coast during a storm three days earlier. Taylor wrote to the Continental Congress, requesting permission to sell the vessel's cargo: "I have orders from General Hugh Mercer to take care of this vessel until further orders. As to the vessel's hull, it lies exposed and is likely to be lost [to] the first eastwardly storm." Though Taylor never received permission to sell the cargo of the *Betsy*, he did so, and probably used the money from the sale to finance his covert activities. Months later, Nathaniel Scudder, writing on behalf of the Monmouth County committee, informed the owners of the *Betsy* that the ship was empty and the whereabouts of its cargo unknown. Scudder blamed George Taylor for the theft of the cargo, stating, "Coll. George Taylor, in whose charge it was [to guard the *Betsy*] and who has proven himself a traitor to his country, & who is gone over to the Enemy, seized the whole of said cargo in the name of the King."

George Taylor's Loyalist activities could not remain secret forever, and as the months passed, he became more publicly disaffected. On November 19, Taylor sent an angry letter to the New Jersey legislature in which he complained that the militia was falling apart around him. He also railed against a recent act of the New Jersey legislature that required all militia officers to take a loyalty oath to the New Jersey government as a condition of holding a commission. Taylor flatly refused the oath, stating:

> As to my part, Gentlemen, I don't choose to qualify for several reasons, and if officers have no other principles to bind them but oaths, I should be very doubtful whether any extraordinary matter might be expected of them. This subject I shall drop, and request information as to whether you choose my resignation or [if] I must act as usual. This, Gentlemen, is in your breasts.

After discussing the deteriorating situation and the controversy surrounding his commission, Taylor concluded the letter ominously: "I shall now remain inactive until I hear from you." George Taylor placed himself in limbo, neither completely leaving the Whig militia nor taking the oath necessary to maintain his commission. Whatever moral high ground Taylor claimed in his letter, it is likely that his ambiguous status was largely the result of a desire to keep his options open.

Taylor's decision to become inactive further disoriented the Monmouth militia. Two days later, Lieutenant Colonel Samuel Forman wrote the legislature urging it to quickly act on Taylor's ambiguous stance. Forman laid out the situation: "There is a task laid before me that I don't like. Col. Taylor refuses taking the oath required: in consequences thereof, the officers refuse to act under him. They request me to take command the next month, which begins tomorrow." Forman declared his willingness to take control of the militia but only after being given orders and a promise of money and provisions from the state commissary. He concluded, "You see the immediate necessity of orders being sent, or our guards on the shore will be suffering for provisions, and in the greatest confusion." Yet Forman's letter apparently went unanswered as it arrived at the same time that the New Jersey government was dissolving in the face of the British invasion of New Jersey.

George Taylor's ambiguous status could not last long, especially once Colonel David Forman (cousin of Samuel Forman) returned to Monmouth County on November 24, 1776. David Forman's mission was to lead his regiment of Continental soldiers home and round up its Loyalist leaders.

David Forman arrested nearly one hundred Monmouthers. He wrote to George Washington that he was hoping to capture William and George Taylor. William Taylor (George's cousin) later wrote, "They [Forman's party] took nearly 100 of his [Taylor's] relatives, who were removed 300 miles to Fredericktown [Frederick, Maryland]." On November 28, George Taylor, likely fearing capture, left Monmouth County and became a Loyalist refugee.

Three weeks later, George Taylor was recommissioned as colonel of the Monmouth County militia, though this time it was under the authority of the royal governor, William Franklin, in the service of the king. With his new commission, George Taylor returned home and played an active role in rallying support for the county's newly formed Loyalist regime, headed by his uncle, John Taylor. Yet this so-called Loyalist ascendancy was short-lived. On January 2, 1777, a party of Pennsylvania Continentals dispersed the newly formed Loyalist militia (see chapter 5 for a more complete discussion of the Pennsylvania Continentals' campaign in Monmouth County).

General Courtland Skinner, commanding New Jersey's Loyalist forces from New Brunswick, ordered George Taylor to stand alone with his disintegrating Loyalist militia against the Continentals. Skinner noted that he had ordered the Loyalists already mustered into the New Jersey Volunteers to join him in New Brunswick. But Skinner was not prepared to give up Monmouth County: "You [George Taylor] are therefore to muster the Militia and take such part as will prevent small parties from entering the County, and distressing the People." A month later, Skinner again ordered Taylor into Monmouth County to revive the broken Loyalist regime. Taylor's orders read, "It will be very proper, upon entering the County, to summon the inhabitants without distinction to renew their oaths and fidelity, and form them into such companies for the purpose of expelling the enemy and afterwards keeping the County." There is no reason to think that Taylor was able to muster many men or offer any significant resistance.

EDWARD AND GEORGE TAYLOR AS ACTIVE LOYALISTS

By the spring of 1777, Edward Taylor had been arrested for opposing the New Jersey government, and George Taylor was in the military service of the king. While Edward chose to stay at home, his Loyalist sympathies kept him from weathering the war easily. For George, the war offered an opportunity to seek military glory and work for the restoration of British rule. Yet despite residing on different sides of enemy lines, the lives of Edward and George Taylor grew more intertwined.

Though Edward Taylor did not turn refugee and join the British, he was far from a dutiful citizen of the new government. On April 14, 1777, Edward Taylor was brought before the Monmouth County committee on charges of refusing to accept Continental money for payment of a debt. In refusing this money, Taylor could have argued that he was just exercising sound business judgment. Continental currency was wildly inflationary, and many creditors refused the new paper money. But William Bostwick and Zephanniah Morris gave depositions against Taylor that accused him of speaking ill of the government while refusing the Continental money. On April 17, David Forman gave a deposition in which he accused Edward Taylor of taking loyalty oaths to the British government and refusing "to take on oaths to the State of New Jersey." With the three depositions in hand, the New Jersey government prosecuted Edward Taylor as an enemy of the state.

Edward Taylor was summoned to appear before the New Jersey Council of Safety to answer charges for being "disaffected and dangerous to the Government." The council offered Edward Taylor parole without further punishment on the condition that he sign a loyalty oath to the new government. But Taylor refused the oath and was only released after Joseph Borden and William Imlay posted £300 bonds to the state, pending Edward Taylor's good behavior and appearance at the next session of the

REVOLUTIONARY WAR CURRENCIES

During the war years and until the adoption of the federal Constitution, the Continental and state governments printed their own currencies in addition to issuing various notes and bonds. The money, rarely backed by gold and silver, was wildly inflationary and used only reluctantly by many. Because of the resulting instability in New Jersey (and elsewhere), most financial records were kept in English pounds and were based on the value of British-backed currency printed in New York.

Monmouth Court of Oyer and Terminer. The help from his friends was an act of kindness that was soon reciprocated. Edward Taylor posted £300 bonds for the release of two similarly disaffected neighbors on April 26 and 27. These actions prove that Edward Taylor was not only disaffected but also unashamed to associate with other disaffected Monmouthers.

While Edward Taylor struggled through the spring, George Taylor spent those same months leading a group of Monmouth Loyalists, the remnants of the Loyalist militia he attempted to form during the Loyalist ascendency. On February 26, Cortland Skinner authorized Taylor to return to Monmouth County, reassemble the Loyalist militia and issue Loyalty oaths. Taylor apparently went to Sandy Hook and began his career as a Loyalist partisan. By June, George Taylor was operating out of Sandy Hook, opposite the Monmouth County militia he had commanded just eight months earlier. That June, he led four expeditions into Monmouth County to punish his enemies and encourage additional disaffected Monmouthers to join his Loyalists at Sandy Hook.

On June 1, George Taylor led a party into Shrewsbury but was attacked by the local militia, and his party suffered the loss of two killed and one captured. Two weeks later, on June 16, George Taylor led a party of Loyalists against the house of Lieutenant Colonel Thomas Seabrook near Point Comfort. Seabrook had become an object of Loyalist resentment because he had signed a British loyalty oath during the Loyalist insurrection, only to revert to being a vigorous Whig when the British pulled back. Taylor's goal was Seabrook's capture, but Seabrook was not at home when the Loyalists arrived. So Taylor's party compensated by plundering Seabrook's house and barn of £31 worth of food stored for the militia, including ten hams and various household items. When Seabrook's son, Stephen, protested, he was bayoneted. Compared to the brutality that characterized the later years of the war in Monmouth County, this incident seems trivial, but it was one of the first cases of true retributive violence in Monmouth County, and it enraged local Whigs. It is unclear whether George Taylor approved the wounding of young Seabrook, but as the expedition's leader, Taylor was seen as responsible.

On June 21, George Taylor led a third expedition into Monmouth County—against Middletown—with the goal of carrying off supplies to the Loyalists on Sandy Hook. It appears that George Taylor and his men spent some time in Middletown visiting with kin and friends, and George visited with his father, Edward. Taylor's party was discovered, and the party was nearly captured when it was attacked by a militia party led by David Forman (now a general in the New Jersey Militia). In the skirmish that followed, four of Taylor's men were killed or captured, but the rest escaped back to Sandy Hook via Edward Taylor's property. The escape route was apparently prearranged. Edward Taylor's fence rails were removed before George Taylor's party arrived, allowing the Loyalists to drive off with a wagon full of provisions as they fled. Interestingly, Edward Taylor's decision to remove his fence rails aroused concern among the Whigs even before George Taylor took advantage of the breach. A few days prior to the raid, Stephen Seabrook (the same man wounded by George Taylor's party) confronted Edward Taylor about the fence rails. Seabrook recalled:

> *I went in company with James Kelsey & we came to the fence Edward Taylor had cut, with his axe [still] in his hand. Upon our coming to him, a conversation began, me & the sd. Taylor, about the fence and land. I told Taylor it was poor business. Taylor acknowledged he had cut 20 or 30 panel & he would be damned if it was put up again.*

Only three days later, George Taylor made yet another descent into Monmouth County. This time, his party penetrated as far as Freehold, probably in an attempt to capture David Forman. The mission was not successful, and Taylor's party was again forced to flee to its boats. As the Loyalists waded out to their boats, a militia party under David Forman arrived and started firing. Forman described the event in a letter printed in the *Pennsylvania Packet*:

> *I laid the bait Saturday to break up the plundering of Colonel George Taylor; it so far succeeded that I was within an Ace of taking the whole [party]; we took one white man and one Negro. While the rest were swimming toward a boat that was coming to take them off, we fired upon them, and killed one and wounded another, who were both hauled into the boat.*

This second near-capture likely convinced George Taylor to change his tactics. It was years before he again led a military expedition into Monmouth County, though he did, apparently by himself, return to Middletown to visit his father in July.

"I Am as Innocent as an Unborn Child"

Unable to capture the elusive George Taylor, David Forman turned his attention to Edward Taylor. On July 2, Edward Taylor received a letter from David Forman accusing him of "acting as a Spy amongst us…and giving intelligence to a party of Tories and British, commanded by your son, late the militia Coll., now a refugee, by which means the party escaped the pursuit of a party of Militia sent to attack them." With Edward Taylor's complicity apparent to Forman, Edward Taylor was put under house arrest. Forman ordered Edward Taylor to "confine yourself to your farm at Middletown, and do not re-attempt to travel the road more than crossing it to go to your land on the north side of said town." A month later, Edward Taylor protested his punishment in a letter to the New Jersey legislature, writing, "The charges against me are intirely [*sic*] unjust. I am as innocent as an unborn child." Taylor complained that the punishment of house arrest was also crippling his economic life:

> *Tho' innocent, I strictly obey the orders of confinement which is a considerable damage to me and my business, having a grist mill two or three miles from where I live, and nobody but servants to attend her, who I cannot trust without being there.*

Forman's action was the culmination of his built-up animosity toward Edward and George Taylor, but the general's act was without any due process of the law. The New Jersey legislature eventually summoned David Forman to explain his conduct regarding Edward Taylor and a number of other controversies. On November 9, 1777, David Forman resigned his general's commission in the New Jersey Militia rather than answer the complaints against him. Nevertheless, the punishment that Forman imposed on Edward Taylor was upheld. So Edward Taylor endured months of house arrest without trial.

By the summer of 1777, the Loyalist activities of Edward and George Taylor were in decline. For Edward Taylor, the months of legal punishments and social ostracism effectively retired him from public life. For George Taylor, the unsuccessful military forays into Monmouth County apparently convinced him that the dangerous business of partisan warfare was best left to others. While both Edward and George continued to be involved in the intrigues of the war, they were never again as active as they were in the first half of 1777.

EDWARD AND GEORGE TAYLOR DURING THE LATER YEARS OF THE REVOLUTION

Despite their best efforts, Edward and George Taylor failed in their attempts to weaken the new Whig government. Whatever influences Edward once had among his neighbors was gone. He was now an outcast, enduring months of house arrest in his home, Marlpit Hall. Meanwhile, George Taylor's attempts to capture leading Whigs Thomas Seabrook and David Forman were both unsuccessful. And his recruiting efforts were probably similarly disappointing. George Taylor remained the colonel of a nonexistent Loyalist militia while other Loyalist recruiters were rewarded with officers' commissions in the New Jersey Volunteers. Yet even while George and Edward Taylor slowed as active Loyalists, their activities did not entirely stop.

Though under house arrest, Edward Taylor did not stay out of trouble with the New Jersey government. On November 26, 1777, the New Jersey Council of Safety issued a summons for his arrest, and Edward Taylor went before that body in Princeton on December 1. Edward Taylor was (again) found guilty of disaffection. Two days later, the council declared:

> *That Edward Taylor give a bond of £100 to stay within a mile of the College of Princeton, & not depart beyond this limit, and shall be set at liberty when Thos. Canfield, a prisoner at New-York, shall be discharged by the Enemy and suffered to return home.*

Taylor's unusual sentence resulted from the belief that he was communicating with the enemy from his house in Middletown. But the link between Taylor's sentence and the imprisonment of Thomas Canfield, a leading New Jersey Whig who had been recently kidnapped, suggests the sentence had a great deal to do with larger war-related events as well.

Edward Taylor remained on parole in Princeton until May 27, 1778, when he petitioned the legislature to allow him to return home temporarily. The legislature granted him three weeks' leave under the condition that he sign an oath "pledging his faith and Honour not to do or say anything contrary to the interests of the United States." The order also stated that Taylor return under bond to Princeton "unless he shall in the mean time procure the releasement of John Willett, now a prisoner in New-York." On June 13, 1778, the New Jersey legislature officially freed Edward Taylor and commended him for having successfully "procured the release of John

Willett." However, Taylor's freedom was conditional, pending his good behavior and the continued freedom of Willett.

Meanwhile, George Taylor continued to intermingle with Loyalist irregulars in and around Sandy Hook, though there is little evidence that he continued to lead raids. In August 1777, he warned General Cortland Skinner of a collection of Whig boats at Middletown Point and requested troops to lead an attack against them. The request was declined because Skinner had no extra resources. Yet George Taylor's connections inside Monmouth County remained viable. In April 1778, he was sent "six packets and 12 loose Acts of Parliament" to circulate among the disaffected of Monmouth County. On July 5, George Taylor was sent to round up the exhausted and abandoned horses of the British army, left at the Navesink Highlands following the British evacuation to New York after the Battle of Monmouth, fought a week earlier.

A year later, George Taylor resumed a more active posture. On June 5, 1779, he was commissioned to raise a company of Loyalist militia "for the defence of Sandy Hook," with his pay contingent on the number of men he might eventually raise. Soon after, he again led an expedition into Monmouth County, probably to recruit for his new company. He also participated in organizing and equipping the various groups of Loyalists who regularly raided the Monmouth countryside from Sandy Hook, beginning in 1779. In June 1780, George Taylor and Andrew Skinner coauthored a map for General Sir Henry Clinton entitled "The Refugee Posts." The map shows a number of points in the New York City area where Loyalist irregulars operated. Taylor's coauthorship of the map shows that George Taylor was well acquainted with the various raiding activities and partisans in the Greater New York City area.

On August 1, George Taylor attempted his boldest and, in retrospect, most foolish expedition into Monmouth County. He landed near Shrewsbury, under a white flag, with a small party of Monmouth Loyalists. His party included the notorious Chrineyonce Van Mater and Anthony Woodward—both men wanted for participating in the robberies and kidnappings of Whigs years earlier. The *New Jersey Journal* reported the results:

> On Sunday last, eight of the infamous Refugees, five of whom pretended to be officers in the Tyrant's service, were brought to the Commissary of Prisoners at Elizabeth Town, from Monmouth. When they were captured they pleaded they came over with a Flag, and produced their orders; but

> *their frivolous pretensions would not answer their ends, and they are sent to*
> *Philadelphia, to occupy a corner in the new Gaol, until exchanged.*

Subsequent reports on the incident reveal that the militiamen who apprehended the Loyalists searched their luggage and discovered large quantities of counterfeit Continental money. It is probable that George Taylor intended to use this bogus currency to buy foodstuffs and other supplies while in Monmouth County and, upon his return, sell them to the British commissary at Sandy Hook for specie. Taylor's party was found guilty on several charges and jailed.

In a bizarre postscript to this incident, the Monmouth militia party assigned to secure Taylor's luggage proceeded to plunder the possessions and spend the counterfeit currency. The result was a string of court-martials, including Lieutenant John Tice and Ensign Barnes Bennett, whose case was reported in the *New Jersey Gazette*. Bennett was charged with

> *disobeying orders with regard to the trunks and other things brought from*
> *Staten Island with Coll. George Taylor, for suffering the goods to be*
> *embezzled, and passing the counterfeit money which came over under the*
> *said Flag.*

The officers were ultimately found guilty and "cashiered" (dishonorably discharged) from the Monmouth County militia. The scandalous conduct of Taylor's captors probably damaged Whig government in Monmouth County more than any of Taylor's expeditions.

In deciding to spread counterfeit money, George Taylor may have been moved to desperation by the confiscation of his Middletown estate a year earlier. On May 14, 1779, the Court of Common Pleas issued the following order on George Taylor's estate:

> *Final Judgment is had pursuant to Law, against George Taylor (son of*
> *Edward), late of the Township of Middletown, on the inquisition found*
> *against said George Taylor for joining the Army of the King of Great Britain*
> *and otherwise offending…* [the] *Commissioners* [of Confiscations] *are*
> *therefore commanded and enjoined to sell and dispose of the Estate.*

George Taylor had probably hoped to hold onto his estate, since his wife, Deborah, and children remained at the family farm long into the war. According to tax ratables after the confiscation, Deborah went from being the owner of a 220-acre estate to being only a householder (meaning she owned a house but no appreciable amount of land), a steep step down in both wealth and status.

George Taylor did not stay in prison long. He was quickly exchanged for Whig prisoners and returned to New York. In early 1781, George Taylor helped arrange the exchange of two Monmouth Whigs—Daniel Covenhoven and Cornelius Swart. Swart deposed that while captured in New York,

> *George Taylor took them before the commanding officer, he was told by Taylor that he [Taylor] could discharge them if he thought proper—at which Taylor told them that he paroled them both to return home and remain peaceable subjects.*

In arranging this release, Taylor may have been paying back a favor owed to Whig families who had used their influence to have him quickly exchanged, though this cannot be proven. That spring, George Taylor probably participated in the massive June 1781 raid of Middletown. This is likely because the raid was led by his longtime sponsor, Courtland Skinner, and the raiders razed the Baptist meetinghouse, the same religious congregation that had expelled his family.

By 1782, George Taylor was living peacefully in New York, but he apparently remained active in the London trade that went on between Sandy Hook's Loyalist traders and disaffected Monmouthers. On January 9, 1782, Tunis Swart, a London trader, was captured with a barge full of flour. Swart confessed "that he was going to land it [his cargo] for George Taylor." Taylor was also implicated in the London trading of Nathan Jackson, a duplicitous Yankee privateer who apparently faked the capture of his vessels by the British as part of a scheme for bringing goods to New York. Taylor's last documented act during the war was signing a petition in July 1782 protesting the capture and imprisonment of Ezekiel Tilton, another Monmouth Loyalist.

Life in Monmouth County was difficult for George Taylor's family. His considerable estate of 220 acres, two slaves and eleven head of livestock was confiscated, and his wife, Deborah, lost the land and livestock on which she was dependent. Deborah was also convicted of a misdemeanor, probably linked to abetting the Loyalist activities of her husband or for protesting the loss of her property. George and Deborah Taylor's adult daughter, Sarah, married John Hagerty, a noncommissioned Virginia Continental soldier who was stationed in Monmouth County in 1779—an enormous drop in status.

George Taylor's postwar life is largely a mystery. He was one of only six Monmouth Loyalists granted a pension by the British government for his civil government service but was denied a military pension after Oliver DeLancey (a leading New York Loyalist) wrote a letter suggesting that his irregular service was not adequate for a military officer's pension. This suggests that Taylor made both friends and enemies among the most influential Loyalists. George Taylor settled in Canada after the war, but because there were many Loyalists named George Taylor, it is not apparent exactly where or whether his wife and younger children joined him.

For Edward Taylor, the last years of the war were equally hard. A vigilante Whig party threatened to burn his house once, and he endured harassments from the same Whig neighbors who had showed him great deference before the war. Court records reveal that Edward Taylor was frequently at odds with his Whig neighbors. In July 1779, he filed suit before the Court of Common Pleas, accusing Peter Schenck, the local magistrate, of trespassing. In December 1781, Edward Taylor was brought before the Court of Oyer and Terminer and charged with perjury; he was found not guilty. Edward Taylor's health started failing him, prompting him to compose his will. In his last will and testament, Edward left nothing to his eldest son, George, despite reportedly being "on affectionate terms with him." George was omitted because, as a Loyalist refugee, any property left to him was subject to confiscation by the New Jersey government upon Edward's death.

Edward Taylor kept much of his estate, despite having parts of it "applied to Publick use"—meaning that Whig troops were supplied from and quartered on his property. As compensation, Taylor was paid in virtually worthless Continental vouchers. Edward Taylor's considerable business interests suffered because of his loyalism, and his prosperous estate, listed in the 1778 tax rolls as 1,200 acres, two slaves and forty-two head of livestock, fell to 430 acres, one slave and twenty livestock by 1783, the year of his death. So while Edward Taylor remained comfortable, he slipped from the ranks of the county's handful of wealthiest. Two of Edward's younger children, John and Sarah, also apparently did not fare well during the war. John Taylor served in the Loyalist New Jersey Volunteers briefly early in the war and weathered the rest of the war apparently as a nonparticipant. His small estate, 24 acres in both 1778 and 1783, indicates a modest existence below the station that he might have expected had his father's prominence not fallen. Edward's daughter, Sarah, married John Nivison in 1781, a modest Whig with only a 21-acre estate, again indicating a substantial step down in status and wealth.

MONMOUTH COUNTY'S OTHER WHIG-LOYALIST LEADERS

The Taylors are an excellent case study for demonstrating how the Revolution impacted a bloc of Monmouth County's prewar leaders—early Whigs who became Loyalists. Evidence of other prewar leaders turning Loyalist is best demonstrated in Middletown Township, where the fortunate preservation of the prewar *Town Book* makes it possible to know the town's prewar

TABLE 1: MIDDLETOWN'S PRE-WAR LEADERS WHO LEANED TOWARD DISAFFECTION

NAME	LEADERSHIP POSITION	EVIDENCE OF DISAFFECTION
Grover, James, Esq.	county freeholder; justice of the courts; delegate to provincial convention	Issues loyalty oaths for British during Loyalist insurrection; refuses summons from New Jersey Council of Safety
Grover, John	member of Township Committee	Disarms Whigs during Loyalist insurrection
Hartshorne, Essek	county assessor	Arrest warrant issued April 1777 by New Jersey Council of Safety; refuses loyalty oath to Whig government
Hendrickson, Daniel (of Middletown)	commissioner of appeals; township collector; overseer of the poor	Arrest warrant issued April 1777 by New Jersey Council of Safety
Kearney, Revaud	port collector	Signs anti-independence petition; condemns Whigs; shelters Loyalist partisans
Kearney, Thomas	surveyor	Implicated in London trade; shelters Loyalists
Taylor, Edward	delegate, New Jersey Assembly and Provincial Congress; committeeman	Refuses to sign resolution supporting Continental Congress; refuses loyalty oath; refuses Continental money
Taylor, John	justice of the courts; sheriff; delegate, Provincial Convention	Arrest warrant issued by Whig government; high commissioner for issuing oaths during Loyalist insurrection; signs public notice for Loyalist regime
Van Mater, John	militia captain; committeeman	Participates in the arrest of Whigs during Loyalist insurrection
Wardell, Henry	attorney; militia captain	Resigns from militia when British land at Sandy Hook; seizes county records during Loyalist insurrection

officeholders (comparable documentation does not exist for Monmouth's other five townships). Ten of the twenty-nine men who held office in Middletown between 1770 and early 1776 became disaffected toward the Whig government. It is noteworthy that eight of these ten disaffected leaders suffered considerable drops in personal wealth during the war versus only eight of the nineteen prewar leaders who became Whigs. In an area where many were plundered, being a prominent Whig might cause economic misfortune at the hands of Loyalist raiders, but the systematic punishments visited upon the disaffected made that outcome a near-certainty.

The removal of one-third of Middletown's prewar leaders demonstrates that the fall of Edward and George was not unique. Outside of Middletown, prewar leaders from other Monmouth townships—including Justice of the Peace Joseph Throckmorton, Justice of the Courts John Wardell, Sheriff Elisha Lawrence, Assemblyman Robert Hartshorne, Surveyor Richard Lawrence, Lieutenant Colonel Thomas Salter, Reverend Samuel Cooke and Captain John Longstreet—prove that many others followed the same ruinous Whig-to-Loyalist path as the Taylors.

CONCLUSION

The story of Edward and George Taylor during the American Revolution illustrates the ruinous side of the American Revolution for a prominent family at the forefront of local leadership prior to the war. On the one hand, the Taylors were victims. Edward Taylor endured numerous punishments for his political views, and George was driven into exile and lost his property. Their families also suffered. But the Taylors, despite Edward's protests, were not as innocent as unborn children. Edward Taylor opposed the laudable ideals of the Revolution and the democratic initiatives of the Provincial Congress; he also abetted Loyalist activities after taking oaths that he would not do so. George led men in plundering raids against his former neighbors and was party to various brutal and provocative acts. It is no coincidence that the Taylors crossed from Whig to Loyalist at the low-water mark of the American Revolution, as the British army pushed into and took control of much of New Jersey in the latter part of 1776. This suggests a confluence of ideology with calculated self-interest.

In 1774, the Taylors' Whig views put them at the center of local anti-British agitation. But as their neighbors gradually came to embrace the concept of rebellion, the Taylors' views shifted on the political spectrum primarily because the spectrum itself shifted radically between 1774 and 1776. By 1777, Edward and George Taylor had turned from leading the agitation against British authority to risking their property and lives in hopes of preserving that same authority. The reversal might seem complete and sudden, but it was not. For Edward and George Taylor, denouncing particular policies and assembling men to better coordinate dissent was a perfectly acceptable course of action for a loyal citizen of a beneficent king being duped by manipulative ministers. Such actions were well within the boundaries established by a century of Whig agitation in England. However, leading those same men in forming a new government or into battle against the king's troops was unacceptable because it unambiguously crossed into the realm of treason. Like the Girondists of the French Revolution, Edward and George Taylor and the other Whig-Loyalists paid dearly for the reforms they espoused and the Revolution they opposed.

The sad story of Edward and George Taylor illustrates the line between Whig and Loyalist and how that line changed over time. It also shows that the war changed and damaged lives along the military frontier, even lives of noncombatants. But the Taylors' story is representative of only one kind of Loyalist: the prewar squire who embraced loyalism only after the Whig movement embraced armed rebellion. The next chapter documents Loyalists on the opposite end of the social hierarchy—African American slaves and laborers who embraced loyalism and became a potent force along the military frontier.

This chapter is based on a more detailed essay of the same name that appeared in the journal New Jersey History *in 2005.*

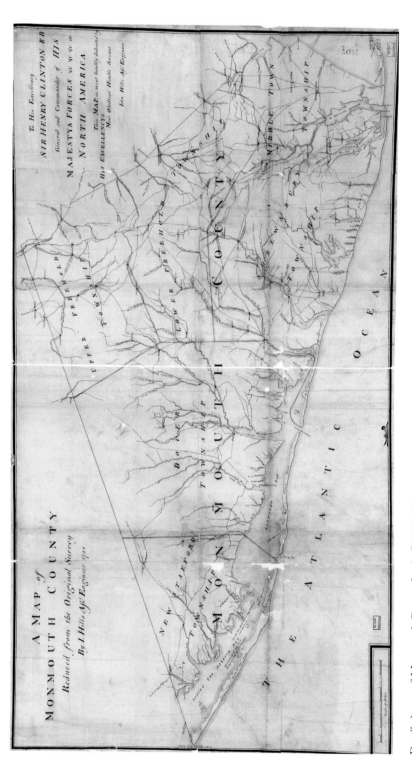

Detailed map of Monmouth County for the British high command, reduced from the original survey. The British chose not to develop such detailed maps for most New Jersey counties. Map drawn by John Hills, 1781; original at the Library of Congress, Washington, D.C. *Courtesy of Library of Congress.*

Christ Church, serving a large Anglican congregation at Shrewsbury. Its minister, Reverend Samuel Cooke, left the church at the start of the war to serve as a chaplain in the British army. *Photo by Michael Adelberg.*

Photo of Marlpit Hall, the home of Edward Taylor, where he was confined under house arrest for many months. It was among the finer homes in Middletown. *Photo by Michael Adelberg.*

Left: The Presbyterian meetinghouse (Old Tennant Church) in Manalapan, used as a militia muster site and as a hospital during the Battle of Monmouth. *Photo by Michael Adelberg.*

Below: Note issued to investors in the Sandy Hook Lighthouse in the 1760s containing the earliest surviving image of the lighthouse. *Courtesy of the United States Lighthouse Society, San Francisco, California.*

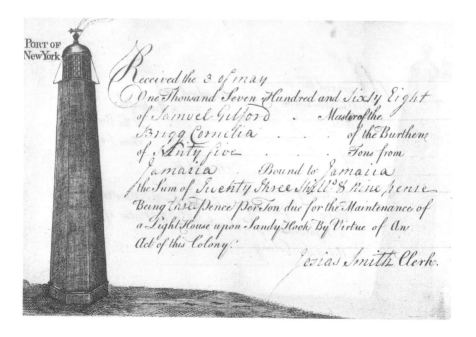

Right: Portrait of Brigadier General David Forman in dress uniform, circa 1784, by Charles Wilson Peale. Note the similarities in appearance with portraits of George Washington from the same period. *Courtesy of the Berkshire Museum, Pittsfield, Massachusetts.*

Below: Drawing of the Monmouth County Courthouse by Carrie Swift, circa 1880, the scene of riotous elections, capital convictions and at least one murder. *Courtesy of the Monmouth County Historical Association, Freehold, New Jersey. Gift of Mrs. Rulif V. Lawrence, 1932.*

Josiah Halstead's tavern (the Allen House), which hosted several contentious meetings as the people of Shrewsbury initially chose not to participate in anti-British dissent. It also hosted Continental soldiers later in the war. *Photo by Michael Adelberg.*

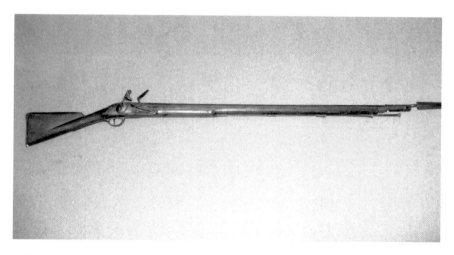

A British musket used during the Battle of Monmouth by Zachariah Hankins after Hankins's own musket was shattered by a musket ball. *Photo by Bernadette Rogoff, courtesy of the Monmouth County Historical Association, Freehold, New Jersey. Gift of Mr. Arthur Hankins, 1992.*

Right: Sketch, Sandy Hook Lighthouse, circa 1790. *Courtesy of the United States Lighthouse Society, San Francisco, California.*

Below: The home of John Burrowes, chairman of the Monmouth County Committee, and John Burrowes Jr., who rose to the rank of major in the Continental army. The home was raided by Loyalists in 1778. *Photo from the Historic American Buildings Survey, Library of Congress, Washington, D.C.*

New Jersey Militia as portrayed by reenactors. Due to uniform shortages early in the war, many Continental army units may have appeared the same. Note that the men are not in formation as they fire. *Photo by Gina Provenzano, Monmouth Battlefield State Park, Manalapan, New Jersey, 2008.*

First Battalion of New Jersey Volunteers reenactors. Originally raised from Monmouth County in 1776, these Loyalists first wore green coats. *Photo by Garry Wheeler Stone, Monmouth Battlefield State Park, Manalapan, New Jersey, 2008.*

4

"A MOTLEY CREW AT SANDY HOOK"

Monmouth's African American Loyalists

By August 1780, Tye, a slave before the war, was a hero to local Loyalists. They awarded him the honorary title of colonel. He was also well known and feared by local Whigs. In the previous five months, Tye had led at least four raids from Sandy Hook into Monmouth County, taken almost two hundred head of livestock and captured several leading citizens, including two New Jersey legislators (James Mott and Hendrick Smock) and two militia officers (Lieutenant Colonel John Smock and Captain Barnes Smock). Tye was leader of a group of runaway slaves called the Black Brigade that camped on Sandy Hook during the warm months and sustained itself by plundering the farms and homesteads of its former masters.

On the evening of August 31, 1780, Tye led a mixed race party of about thirty (some reports indicate the party was larger) on its boldest expedition. His men evaded militia patrols and penetrated fifteen miles inland to the tavern of Joshua Huddy at Colts Neck. Huddy was hated by Loyalists for his role in the 1777 hanging of the Loyalist Stephen Edwards and other provocative acts. Near dawn, Tye's men surrounded the tavern, but Huddy and his mistress, Lucretia Emmons, successfully held off Tye's men by firing several preloaded muskets and then efficiently reloading and refiring the guns. The standoff ended when a raider came in close and put a torch to the tavern. Huddy and Tye negotiated the terms of his surrender: Huddy's capture in exchange for extinguishing the fire and allowing Emmons to escape. The raiders honored the terms of the surrender but then proceeded to sack the tavern and fill their wagons with booty before departing.

The sun was up by the time the raiders made it back to shore and loaded their barges. A party of Salem County militia, helping to protect the vulnerable Monmouth shoreline, and a party of local militia arrived. In the ensuing skirmish, Huddy was shot in the leg, and the barge on which he was detained overset. He swam to shore, shouting, "I am Huddy! I am Huddy!" to distinguish himself from his captors. The raiding party ultimately made its escape with the loss of a few men shot in the skirmish and a few more drowned. Tye was shot in the wrist during the action. The wound became infected, and he died several weeks later. One militiaman was killed and one more wounded. Huddy escaped that day, but he only survived another eighteen months. In March 1782, he was again captured and was hanged two weeks later on the highlands opposite Sandy Hook. His hangman was an African American Loyalist named Moses.

The Declaration of Independence promised Americans the right to "life, liberty, and the pursuit of happiness," but enslaved African Americans saw the Revolutionary cause as one committed to maintaining the tyrannous institution of slavery. When the British offered freedom to slaves who would take up arms against the rebelling Americans, thousands of slaves escaped to join them. In Monmouth County, the difficult prewar relationship between the races, the inability of the Continental army to offer effective assistance against Loyalist raiders (discussed in the next chapter) and the proximity of the British base at Sandy Hook set the stage for African Americans embodying into armed groups and having a significant impact on the local war.

RACIAL DIVISIONS AND CONDITIONS IN PRE-REVOLUTIONARY MONMOUTH COUNTY

The extent of slavery in the areas surrounding New York City prior to the Revolutionary War was far greater than that of any other region north of the Chesapeake. The African American slave population in the Greater New

York City area exceeded 10 percent and was rising (from 10.4 percent of the total population in 1745 to 11.4 percent in 1790). In Monmouth County, the African American population also exceeded 10 percent (an estimated twelve to fourteen hundred people), with approximately one-third free and two-thirds held in slavery. Most were concentrated in the county's two northeastern townships, Shrewsbury and Middletown, where the African American population, both slave and free, was close to 20 percent of the white population. Despite the large numbers, Monmouth County had no large slaveholders; no man owned more than six.

With the help of a sizable Quaker community committed to charity and abolition, several African Americans won their freedom and owned land in Monmouth County. Between 1774 and 1778, Quakers purchased the freedom of or shamed thirty-seven slave owners into freeing their slaves. In Shrewsbury and Upper Freehold Townships, where the Quaker influence was strongest, fourteen African Americans, based on the tax rolls, owned their own homes. However, these individuals were the exception; most African Americans, whether slave or free, lived as poor agricultural laborers on the bottom rung of the colonial social ladder. Free African Americans and mixed race children were disproportionately represented on the rolls of the overseers of the poor.

By the 1770s, Whig arguments against Great Britain focused increasingly on British tyranny against the God-given and inalienable rights of all people. These arguments enlivened the debate on ending slavery, especially as more and more Americans complained about being "slaves" to the British Parliament. Early Whig documents from Monmouth County specifically referred to British attempts to wrestle Americans into slavery. Against this rhetorical backdrop, and spurred on by a politically active Quaker population, the abolition of slavery was a hotly debated topic. For example, a 1773 petition from six New Jersey counties (including Monmouth) to the assembly openly wondered about "the evils arising from human slavery."

In Monmouth County, the intermingling of free and slave African Americans, activist Quakers and slaveholders created a volatile mix. In February 1774, 108 residents of Middletown and Shrewsbury Townships sent three identical petitions to the New Jersey Assembly complaining of slave agitation and arguing against slave manumission. The petitioners noted:

There is a great number of Negro men, women and children being slaves,
and are daily increasing in numbers & impudence, that we find them very

troublesome, by running about at all times of the night, stealing & taking & riding other people's horses & other mischief.

The petitioners argued that free African Americans were the main corrupting influence on the slave population, claiming that the troublesome slaves were unruly "in a great degree owing to their having correspondence and recourse to the houses of them already freed."

Nevertheless, Quakers continued to pressure slaveholders to free their slaves and expelled their own recalcitrant members starting in 1776. In addition, the Friends provided financial assistance and education to freed slaves (including holding onto slave children until their age of majority, creating a difficult situation in which parents were freed but not their children). Meanwhile, more slaveholders were having troubles with their slaves. Robert Hartshorne, for example, reported that his female slave "has misbehaved by having a mulatto child and otherwise has given me much trouble."

The tense racial situation in eastern Monmouth County prompted a backlash. On October 6, 1775, the Shrewsbury committee (acting as the de facto local government due to the breakdown of royal authority) took up the issue of controlling the unruly African American population. After hearing complaints made by slave owners against African Americans, the committee acted:

Ordered, whereas the numerous and riotous meeting of Negroes at unlicensed houses is pernicious in itself and may be of pernicious consequences; if the Coll. [of the militia] *is informed of any such meetings, he is desired to use his militia to secure the Negroes, and give the names of the delinquents* [to this committee].

At its next meeting on October 16, the committee took additional steps:

Whereas the meeting together of servants, Negroes and other disorderly persons at unlicensed taverns and other bad houses is attended with great damage not only to the masters but to all, and may be of more pernicious and fatal consequences to the community, therefore, so that the penalties may be more duly inflicted upon all offenders—Resolved, the Coll. shall order parties of militia to attend such suspected places to search for and apprehend all transgressors of the law.

The militia embodied, and notably, the first campaign of the Whig militia in Monmouth County was not directed against royal authority but against a segment of its own population.

By February 1776, at the same time Whigs throughout the colonies were mustering into the Continental army in defense of American liberty, Monmouth County's Whigs were further checking the liberties of the local African American community, including freed slaves. On February 16, 1776, the Shrewsbury committee took strong action, ordering "that all arms in the hands of or at the disposal of Negroes, either free or slaves, shall be taken and secured by the Militia officers until the present troubles are settled." On February 29, the committee went even further:

> *Resolved, that all servants, either Negroes, mulattos or others that shall be found off their master's premises any time of the night…may be taken up by any person whatsoever, and secured until a fine of ten shillings be paid, and in failure to pay such a fine, the slave shall be delivered to the minute men* [militia] *to be kept under guard until he shall receive lashes on the bare back.*

Thus, by the end of February 1776, the African Americans of eastern Monmouth County (including freed men) were prohibited from assembling, possessing arms and going out at night for any reason. The limitations placed on the inalienable rights of individuals—including free African Americans and persons of mixed race—alienated many local African Americans from the Revolutionary cause.

Exactly what prompted the Monmouth Whigs to take such strong actions against the local African American population remains a frustrating mystery, but the crackdown fits within broader colonial trends. Waves of anti-slave agitation were common in the Greater New York area prior to the Revolution. Gregory Dowd, who has studied African Americans in Revolutionary New Jersey, concluded that a wave of anti–African American sentiment rose in New Jersey shortly after Lord Dunmore (the royal governor of Virginia) promised freedom to all slaves of Whigs who would join the British army in November 1775. It is probable that the actions of the Shrewsbury committee were influenced by news from Virginia. But there can be no doubt that some members of the African American community, perhaps emboldened by the same democratic rhetoric that was inspiring the Whigs, were making provocative statements and showing less deference toward slaveholders. This would explain why the first concern of the Whig committees was stopping African Americans from assembling at "unlicensed houses," where slaveholders could not check the spread of dangerous ideas.

It should also be noted that the Whigs of Monmouth County, though perhaps more zealous than others, were not unique in excluding African Americans from full participation in New Jersey's civil institutions. Though New Jersey's militia law stated that "all able bodied men not being slaves" were to be drawn into militia companies, Robert Gough, who has studied African American participation in the Revolutionary militia, concluded that free African Americans suffered a de facto ban from militia service in many New Jersey counties. Similarly, though one of New Jersey's leading Whigs, Jonathan Sargent, favored mustering free African Americans into a separate force for the defense of New Jersey, he dared not suggest the idea publicly, labeling his own idea "heretical" to the majority of New Jersey Whigs. Thus, there is clear evidence that African Americans, whether slave or free, were often viewed with distrust by New Jersey's emerging Whig leaders (even as the long-term abolition of slavery was being considered by many of the same men).

In December 1776, the British army swept across New Jersey and chased the Continental army into Pennsylvania. Emboldened by the tide of the war, Loyalists in Monmouth County seized control. Several African Americans supported this uprising and suffered in the aftermath. In early 1777, shortly after the Whigs regained control, a slave named Sip warned a group of Whigs not to punish him for his activities during the Loyalist uprising. According to a sworn deposition:

> *The said Negro* [Sip] *supposed that the damn Rebels would soon be after him, but if they did, he would take shot amongst them; Sip at this time had a gun with him, that he got from Peter Wardell, a Refugee Tory.*

In another case, two slaves were arrested for "having been in arms and aiding the Enemy." Two other slaves, Joe and Scipio, were arrested by Captain John Dennis of the Shrewsbury militia "on suspicion of intending to join the enemy." Eventually, William Livingston, the governor of New Jersey, intervened on behalf of the slaves' masters, concluding that "it appears that the suspicions against them [Joe and Scipio] are not well founded." Joe and Scipio were released back into the hands of their masters after spending five months in jail. The tensions of the times probably contributed to other acts of racially motivated violence; John and James Williams, for example, severely beat "through a passion" the freed slave Caesar Moore, an assault for which they were never charged.

By the end of 1776, the Whigs of Monmouth County, and much of New Jersey, had made a conscious decision to exclude African Americans from participation in the Revolutionary cause (this hard line eventually softened, particularly in the Continental army, where many African Americans served). The aggressive actions taken by Monmouth's Whigs embittered many in the local African American community against the Revolutionary movement.

THE LURE OF SANDY HOOK

Even before the war, British navy vessels anchored off Sandy Hook and camped soldiers at its strategically important lighthouse. Despite several attempts to dislodge the British, they held Sandy Hook throughout the war. With British-held Sandy Hook and Staten Island nearby, Monmouth County slaves had the opportunity to take advantage of Governor Dunmore's declaration and seek British refuge. As early as March 1776, Monmouth slaves were running off to the British. Gilbert Longstreet, for example, advertised losing a male slave, Tony Ward, on March 4, 1776. Longstreet indicated that Ward would be difficult to capture because "he passes for a free Negro," suggesting he was heading to eastern Monmouth County (and toward Sandy Hook), where there was a substantial free African American population. Indeed, the presence of a substantial free African American population in eastern Monmouth County probably made it much easier for runaway slaves to move about and escape into British lines.

On June 29, 1776, a large British fleet sailed into New York Harbor and anchored off Sandy Hook. The presence of this fleet inspired many Monmouthers, race notwithstanding, to seek British protection. On July 9, Colonel Daniel Hendrickson of Shrewsbury Township appeared before the New Jersey legislature to request permission to go aboard the British fleet and attempt to recover runaway slaves. Hendrickson "informed the Convention that some Negro slaves had run off, and were on board the enemy's fleet; that he had reason to believe he could recover the slaves if he were permitted to send of Flagg [sic]." Meanwhile, other Monmouthers were also attempting to retrieve runaway slaves, and two Shrewsbury Loyalists, William Corlies and George Allen, reached protection behind British lines after going off to the British under the pretense of retrieving "two Negroes who had run away from William Kipping and John Corlies."

It is impossible to know the precise number of African Americans from Monmouth County who escaped to the British. The documentary evidence is very thin: some newspaper advertisements, some military papers of questionable accuracy and a number of incomplete and sometimes contradictory postwar reports. Collectively, these sources are not likely to capture all of the African Americans (slave and free) who sought British protection.

Yet even with uneven documentary evidence, it is apparent that the exodus of Monmouth County's African Americans to British lines was considerable. At least 37 Monmouth County slaves ran away during the American Revolution, and apparently the majority were adult men. This is a considerable number in a county that likely had only 200 to 250 adult male slaves. It can be assumed that the actual number of runaways was much greater due to the fragmentary nature of the sources available. There were three documented cases of kin running off together—the Jones family, the brothers Vaughan and Harry Covenhoven and Captain Kenneth Hankinson's female slave and her daughter (fathered by Lewis Wolis, a Native American). The flight of slaves from Monmouth County to Sandy Hook began at the onset of the war and continued throughout the war, with at least two slaves running away each year.

Most of the slaveholders who lost slaves were supporters of the Revolution, including leading Whigs Colonel David Forman, Captain Kenneth Hankinson, Captain Benjamin Van Cleaf and Assemblyman John Covenhoven. But others who lost slaves were persons of questionable loyalty, including Abiel Aiken and Samuel Breese (both of whom held local leadership positions in the Whig militia and government but whose loyalty was questioned by other leading Whigs). At least one slaveholder who lost slaves was an outright Loyalist: Samuel Cooke (the Anglican minister at Shrewsbury who eventually served as a chaplain in the British army).

It was commonly supposed that the runaway slaves were headed for British lines. A runaway slave advertisement offering a reward for the return of Mark and Chess posted by Richard Britton, for example, includes the telling phrase: "It is feared they will go off to the enemy."

It is impossible to determine what became of all the runaways when they reached Sandy Hook, but the British did organize many of them into military units. A return of the Black Pioneers, commanded by New Jersey Loyalist

TABLE 2: MONMOUTH COUNTY SLAVES WHO RAN AWAY DURING AMERICAN REVOLUTION

YEAR OF DEPARTURE	NAME (AGE IN PARENS)	TOWNSHIP	SLAVE OWNER
1776	Tony Ward	Shrewsbury	Gilbert Longstreet
1776	Unknown	Shrewsbury	John Corlies
1776	Unknown	Shrewsbury	Daniel Hendrickson
1776	Unknown	Shrewsbury	William Kipping
1776	Unknown	Shrewsbury	Samuel Breese
1777	Aaron Jones (42)	Middletown	Hendrick Smock
1777	Isaac Jones (10)	Middletown	Richard Stout
1777	Sarah Jones (42)	Middletown	Richard Stout
1777	Catherine Van Sayl	Middletown	Unknown
1777	John Van Sayl	Middletown	Unknown
1777	Oliver Vinson (30)	Freehold	John Forman
1778	Ben (22)	Upper Freehold	Elisha Lawrence
1778	Cash	Freehold	Kenneth Hankinson
1778	Diannah (10)	Freehold	Kenneth Hankinson
1778	Dinah	Freehold	Benjamin Van Cleave
1778	Thomas Drake (17)	Middletown	Thomas Thurman
1778	Unknown	Shrewsbury	Obadiah Bowne
1778	Unknown	Shrewsbury	Samuel Breese
1778	Unknown	Shrewsbury	Tunis Dennis
1779	Chess	Upper Freehold	Richard Britton
1779	Mark	Upper Freehold	Richard Britton
1779	John Thomas	Dover	Abiel Aiken
1779	Unknown	Freehold	John Van Horn
1780	Unknown	Middletown	Hendrick Stout
1780	Unknown	Middletown	Hendrick Stout
1780	Unknown	Shrewsbury	Garrett Langston
1781	Unknown	Freehold	David Forman
1781	Unknown	Upper Freehold	John Lloyd
1781	Unknown	Middletown	John Vanderveer
1781	Unknown	Freehold	William Wikoff
1782	William Wright	Shrewsbury	Joseph West
1782	Henry Townup	Middletown	Richard Lesner
1782	Unknown	Shrewsbury	Garrett Longstreet
1782	Unknown	Middletown	Richard Van Mater
1782	Unknown	Shrewsbury	Stephen West
1782	Unknown	Freehold	John Covenhoven
1782	Unknown	Shrewsbury	Richard Crawford
Unknown	Unknown Man	Middletown	Samuel Cooke
Unknown	Unknown Girl	Middletown	Samuel Cooke
Unknown	Unknown	Middletown	Christian Van Mater

*The numbers contained in parentheses indicate the age of the slave, when known, at the time he/she escaped.

Richard Robert Crowe, compiled in August 1780 lists 182 men, 74 women and 73 children in the British service as porters and laborers. The British established two official provincial corps comprising African Americans: the Jamaica Volunteers and the Negro Horse, though there is no evidence of either unit seeing significant military action. By 1779, a group of African

Americans had formed themselves in a military association called the Black Brigade. Not officially part of the British army but certainly countenanced by the British, this organization would make a great impact on the irregular warfare in Monmouth County as it moved to a more brutal stage.

African American Loyalists in Irregular Warfare

Individual African Americans participated in civil warfare in Monmouth County as early as 1777. Historian Graham Hodges suggests that the Battle of the Navesink on February 13, 1777, was the beginning of African American military activities at Sandy Hook. In this action, Monmouth Loyalists guided a battalion of British soldiers in a successful ambush of the Monmouth militia. However, information on these guides is sketchy. But in June 1777, George Taylor led the several small raids from Sandy Hook, and African Americans participated in Taylor's party (see previous chapter). An African American was captured by the Monmouth militia after a skirmish with Taylor's men on June 24; Colonel David Forman reported that his men "took one white man and one Negro" during a skirmish with Taylor's party. A few months later, Richard Crawford of Middletown reported the theft of six horses by two Loyalist refugees, "supposed to be one boy, and one Black boy." Unfortunately, documentation of these early irregular military activities is sparse.

In 1778, runaway African Americans and poor white Loyalist refugees established a settlement on Sandy Hook, known as Refugeetown. Colonel David Forman noted that it was "in the cedars" just below the Sandy Hook Lighthouse and consisted of cabins for "60 or 70 refugees, black and white." Militiaman James Bowne further noted, "The enemy was embedded at Sandy Hook, with Negroes and Tories continually coming out." In the summer, the settlement, particularly when swelled with commerce and additional people, must have been unsavory. A British naval officer dubbed it a "stinking edifice."

As the war dragged on, the African Americans at Refugeetown organized themselves into the Black Brigade. No returns of the group exist from its peak years of 1779 and 1780, but a return for the association was compiled at war's end. It lists the group as being composed of forty-nine men, twenty-three women and six children. The first documented action of the Black Brigade may be provided in the diary of Captain Walter Finney, a Pennsylvania officer whose regiment was detached to eastern Monmouth County in early 1779. On April 5, Finney reported pursuing a small raiding party from the village of Shrewsbury, resulting in the capture of "two Negroes."

African American military activity increased dramatically after that, coinciding with the emergence of Colonel Tye as leader of the Black Brigade. Though there is some dispute about Tye's early life, recent scholarship concludes that Tye was the slave Titus, who ran away from John Corlies of Shrewsbury in November 1775. Tye was probably active in the early irregular military activities around Sandy Hook, though this cannot be proven. Graham Hodges has suggested that Tye acted as a guide to the gangs of white Loyalists (called cowboys) who raided and robbed along the Raritan Bay shore. These forays proved a useful internship for Tye.

In June 1779, Tye and the Black Brigade burst out from Sandy Hook with a flurry of activity unmatched by any other local Loyalist group. Though documentation is uneven, it appears that on June 6, Tye led a party from Sandy Hook into Monmouth County. The *New York Royal Gazette* reported, "On Tuesday the 6th, an inhabitant of said [Monmouth] county was taken off to the enemy by four Negroes." Another raid three days later resulted in five prisoners and several sacked houses. These early actions were rather conventional small raids, resulting in single-home robberies and "man-stealings," but the success of these early raids prompted Tye to attempt more ambitious partisan activities.

On July 20, 1779, Tye led his first major raid. The *New Jersey Gazette* recorded the incident:

> *About fifty Negroes and refugees landed at Shrewsbury, and plundered the inhabitants of nearly eighty head of cattle, about 20 horses and a quantity of wearing apparel and household furniture. They also took William Brindley and Elihu Cook, two of the inhabitants.*

This remarkably successful raid established Tye as Sandy Hook's most capable irregular leader. The party successfully penetrated enemy lines, captured one hundred livestock and carried off two hostages—important bargaining chips in the prisoner of war exchanges and ransoming going on between Monmouth County Whig officers and the Loyalist refugees in New York. Tye's men were not above outright plundering: taking apparel, furniture and other expensive goods of no military value.

Knowing the exact connection between the activities of the Black Brigade and British commanders is impossible, but apparently the British quietly countenanced the raiders. There is no evidence, for example, of Tye ever meeting with or being recognized by British officers or even prominent Loyalists. But it cannot be a coincidence that the Black Brigade reached its maturity (in the summer of 1779) at a time when the British were most active in encouraging slave disaffection. In May 1779, General Henry Clinton issued the Phillipsburg Proclamation, in which the British offered protection for all slaves who would come behind British lines and freedom for any slaves who would take up arms as Loyalists. The Loyalist *New York Gazette* printed the June 30 proclamation, and it was reprinted throughout the summer. Whig newspapers lampooned the British policy of courting African Americans. The following satirical verse in the *New Jersey Journal* is just one example of how Whigs greeted Clinton's proclamation:

> *A proclamation of late he sends,*
> *to the thieves and rogues who are his friends;*
> *Those he invites, with all colours he attacks,*
> *But deference he pays to Ethiopian Blacks*

Interestingly, Clinton quickly issued a supplemental statement to the Phillipsburg Proclamation that white Loyalist opportunists who enslaved or sold runaway slaves reaching British lines would be severely punished. This indicates that some runaway slaves who were inspired to seek their freedom behind British lines met with very unfortunate ends.

There is ample evidence that African Americans participated in many smaller actions from the fall of 1779 into 1780. William Lloyd recorded that "the Negro refugees fired upon a sentinel" at Jumping Point in Shrewsbury Township in 1779. His militia party pursued the partisans, who waded into the Shrewsbury River to make their escape. Samuel Lippincott recalled a separate incident in early 1780:

> *While in his bed, in his residence in Monmouth County, the applicant's residence was plundered by two Black Refugees, who laid ready upon his house and took him out of bed. After having tied his hands behind him, they, in the company of several Tories, conveyed him and two other prisoners, to Sandy Hook.*

"A Motley Crew at Sandy Hook"

William McBride recalled that in 1780, he "marched down to Cedar Bridge in search of Col. Tye who had a party of Negroes and runaways under him and were plundering the inhabitants." If Lloyd, McBride and Lippincott had not lived into the 1830s and applied for pensions (only a fraction of Revolutionary War veterans did), these events would never have been recorded, as they are not corroborated by any other source. Also, in 1779, Abiel Aiken, the magistrate at Toms River, reported detaining "a Negro man who calls himself John Thomas" possessing a quantity of stolen clothes and seventy-nine dollars in currency. Thomas escaped. In February 1780, two African Americans were among three Loyalist guides captured in a daring attempt to help twenty-two British prisoners of war escape from Pennsylvania to British-held New York, via Monmouth County.

As the weather warmed, larger raiding parties formed again. In early April 1780, a mixed race party went into Shrewsbury at night and kidnapped two militiamen. On April 30, the infamous white refugee William Gillian led a mixed race party on a raid that was reported in the *New Jersey Gazette*:

> *A party of Negroes and refugees from Sandy Hook landed at Shrewsbury in order to plunder. During the excursion a Mr.* [John] *Russell, who attempted some resistance, was killed, and his grand child had five balls shot through him but is yet living. Captain Warner…was made a prisoner by these ruffians, but was released by giving them two Joes. This banditti also took off several persons, amongst whom were Captain* [James] *Green and Ensign* [John] *Morris of the Militia.*

In this raiding party were some of the most notorious white Loyalist irregulars, including Gillian, Richard Lippincott and John Farnham, each of whom was implicated in one or more murders, proving that the African American irregulars were associating with Sandy Hook's most dangerous Loyalists. The blending of races in these raiding parties was consistent with the Black Brigade's unofficial nature; white and black Loyalist refugees mixed freely on an ad hoc basis depending on the opportunity.

In the summer of 1780, Tye again led the Black Brigade on raids from Sandy Hook into Monmouth County. On June 9, Tye led a mixed race party on one of the most daring irregular raids of the war. The *New Jersey Gazette* reported:

> *Ty, with his party of about twenty black and whites, took and carried off prisoner, Capt. Barnes Smock and* [Lieutenant] *Gilbert Van Mater; at*

the same time, [the irregulars] *spiked up the iron four-pounder at Capt. Smock's house, but took no ammunition. Two of the artillery horses, and two of Capt. Smock's horses were likewise taken off. The above mentioned Ty is a Negro, who wears the title of Colonel, and commands a motley crew at Sandy Hook.*

The audacity of the raiders and the futility of the militia's response prompted Colonel David Forman to write to Governor William Livingston for assistance. Forman noted that Tye's party defeated "a small [militia] party that were collected at his [Smock's] house for mutual defense—this was done with the sun one hour high, 12 miles from one of the landings." Forman argued that the success of Tye's raiders, who attacked Captain Smock's house in the middle of the day, several miles inside American lines, should "induce your Excellency in establishing a guard [that] will in some measure increase the security of this county." Undaunted by the stationing of more soldiers near Sandy Hook, Tye continued to conduct raids. On June 22, the *New Jersey Gazette* reported:

Yesterday morning, a party of the Enemy, consisting of Tye with 30 Blacks, 36 Queen's Rangers [Loyalists], and 30 Refugee Tories, landed at Conkascung [near the Navesink Highlands]. Then by some means got in between our scouts undiscovered, and went up to Mr. James Mott's, plundered his house, and several of the neighbours houses, of almost everything in them; and carried off the following persons, viz., James Mott, Jonathan Pearce, James Johnson, Joseph Dorsett, William Blair, James Walling, Philip Walling, James Wall, Matthew Griggs, also several Negroes, and a great deal of stock, but all the Negroes, one excepted, and the horse, horned cattle and sheep, were re-taken by our people. We had wounded, Capt. [Thomas] Walling slightly, Lieut. Garret Hendrickson had his arm broken, two privates supposed mortally, and a third [Walter Hyer] slightly, in a skirmish we had with them on their retreat. The enemy acknowledged the loss of seven men, but we think it is much more considerable.

During the raid, the Monmouth militia battled the raiders in hand-to-hand combat. Lieutenant Garret Hendrickson and Private Walter Hyer were wounded from sword blows during the skirmish (Hyer was maimed). James Mott's account of the raid notes that he was plundered of a wide variety of items, including "a Negro boy about 15 years old" valued at £100 (far more than any other lost possession). This suggests that the Black Brigade captured, and perhaps liberated, other slaves.

That Tye's party lost much of its booty to the pursuing militia party likely induced Tye to launch another raid a few days later. Militiaman Benjamin Van Cleave recorded a skirmish near Shrewsbury on June 25. Van Cleave recalled that he "was in quite a smart engagement with a band Refugees, headed, or said to be headed, by a Negro called Colonel Tye."

After June, Tye may have become inactive, or his actions simply went unrecorded for a while. But the activities of African American refugees did not cease just because Tye was less active. Twice in late July, African Americans participated in incursions deep into Monmouth County, once penetrating twenty miles inland to Freehold, the county seat and the stronghold of Monmouth's Whigs. Colonel Samuel Forman briefly discussed these two actions in a letter to the governor, writing on August 6, "In two skirmishes last week, our men retook the horses that the enemy took from the neighbourhood of Monmouth Court House, and wounded one Negro." Though not entirely successful, it should be noted that these raids were among the boldest irregular actions of the war, given the long distance inland that the raiders had to travel and the strength of the militia near the county seat.

In August, a party led by Tye succeeded in carrying off two more leading Whigs: Lieutenant Colonel John Smock and Hendrick Smock (a member of the New Jersey General Assembly). The kidnappings may have been a deliberately calculated blow against the Retaliators, the recently created vigilante group established to punish Loyalists. A Loyalist newspaper account of the raid happily noted that John Smock "was of the Associated Community of Retaliators" in its report of the incident (see chapter 6 for more on the Retaliators). By this time, the notoriety of Tye may have broken the spirit of certain militia companies. A return for a class (half of a company) of militia drawn up on August 17 shows that only two of the seventeen militiamen listed on the return—Joseph and Thomas West—responded to the alarm "to March after Colo. Tye." Tye's reputation had reached the point that many militiamen were unwilling to face him.

Two weeks later, Tye led the raid against Colts Neck summarized at the start of this chapter. One of Monmouth's leading Whigs, Nathaniel Scudder, described the action in a letter to his son:

On Saturday night, a party of Refugees came as high as Colts Neck and took Captain Huddy, with loss of one of their party, killed three [militia], & it is said that Colo. Tye being wounded in the wrist—their design was to surprise the guard at Colts Neck...I hear that a party of Middletown militia waylaid the Enemy on their retreat, and fired on them in their boats with such effect that a considerable number, at least eight or nine, were killed, and one of their boats overset, in which Captain Huddy happened to be, by which means he made his escape and swam to shore, having however received a ball from our people in the thigh.

Tye died from his wound weeks later.

With Tye dead, the Black Brigade lost momentum. Graham Hodges noted that West Indian–born Stephen Blueke replaced Tye as leader of the Black Brigade, but there is no evidence that Blueke led any significant raids into Monmouth County. Even with the diminishment of the Black Brigade, individual African American partisans were certainly active after Tye's death. In late 1780, a small party of African American refugees landed at Long Branch, where they were surprised by a militia party. In the mêlée that followed, the so-called Negro's Hill Massacre, all of the Loyalists were bayoneted to death except one. The lone survivor, Sam, a former slave of the Woolley family, survived by feigning death after being stabbed many times. Sam was found nearly dead the next day and was taken back to the Woolley homestead, where he recovered and spent the rest of his life as a slave. Edwin Woolley, a boy at the time, later recalled that Sam "carried with him to the grave, the marks of eleven bayonet wounds on his hands and breast."

The tide of war turned against the African American irregulars at Sandy Hook in 1781 with the emergence of Whig privateers in Raritan Bay who were unafraid of the weakening British naval presence at Sandy Hook. The daring Whig privateer Adam Hyler of New Brunswick showed a particular interest in capturing and selling African American Loyalists. In June 1781, Hyler and his crew captured an African American irregular named Prime while he was camped at Sandy Hook. Prime was sold for thirty pounds, ten shillings—a handsome price. Another African American irregular, York, was captured by Massachusetts privateer Captain William Gray in 1782. Most significantly, Hyler succeeded in capturing the Loyalist vessel *Alert*, with a forty-six-man crew (eleven of whom were African American Loyalists), on April 20, 1782. In his letter to the New Jersey governor describing the capture, it was noted that the white Loyalist prisoners were being brought to

Elizabethtown for prisoner exchange, but "the eleven Negroes are detained for trial" at Admiralty Court, proving that African American partisans were not afforded the same treatment as white Loyalists and could be condemned to Whig privateers as war booty. Finally, Hyler also captured an African American Loyalist, John Jeffrey, while "on board a schooner" near Sandy Hook's fishing banks, suggesting that Hyler was not above kidnapping Loyalists engaged (at least at the moment) in peaceful pursuits.

Several other captured African Americans ended up in Whig prisons and stood trial for felonies. In November 1780 and again in February 1781, four African American and a few white partisans escaped from the jails at Trenton and Freehold, the latter by "sawing off the irons and window gates." Three of the escapees were awaiting execution for stealing horses; the fourth escapee was an African American Loyalist named DeNight who was recaptured soon after the jailbreak. On June 4, 1782, the Monmouth County Court of Oyer and Terminer convicted an African American named Jacob of murder and sentenced him to death. He was hanged later that month. The same court convicted another African American, Jube, for murder as well.

African American Loyalists stayed active into the spring of 1782. On March 24, a one-hundred-man raiding party under the auspices of the Associated Loyalists landed at Toms River, defeated the Whig garrison at the Block House fort and razed the village. The raiding party was described by militiaman George Parker as "a party of Negroes, refugees and sailors," at least one of whom behaved brutally after the battle. Daniel Randolph, a resident of Toms River, noted that "after quarter was called and the Block House surrendered, this deponent saw a Negro, one of the Refugee Party, bayonet Major John Cook." On March 29, a few days later, a small party of Loyalist raiders "weighed anchor from Sandy Hook and passed down to Long Branch," where they were captured. The five-person party included two African Americans, Moses and Isaac.

The last major action involving African American partisans in Monmouth County occurred on June 1, 1782. The *New Jersey Gazette* recorded the action:

One Davenport, a refugee, landed with about 40 Blacks and 40 whites, at Forked River, and burnt Samuel Brown's saltworks, and plundered him; they then proceeded southward toward Barnegat, for purposes of burning the saltworks along the shore between those places.

However, at their second landing, Davenport's party was surprised by a militia detachment in a gunboat that fired at close range, killing Davenport. In the panic that followed, one of the refugees' barges overturned. The raiders and Pine Robbers fled into the woods, though they likely outnumbered the militia party. The debacle at Barnegat is the last recorded action of the African American partisans, save the capital conviction of an African American, Jacob, for murder later that month.

It is impossible to know what became of all of Sandy Hook's African American irregulars after the war. Several participated in the Loyalist resettlements to Canada in 1783. An April 1783 document lists forty-nine men, twenty-three woman and six children from the Black Brigade boarding the *L'Abondance* for settlement in Nova Scotia, and an October 1783 document lists another party of Black Pioneers being settled in Canada. Others stayed in the New York area. By 1784, slaves composed only 4.3 percent of Shrewsbury Township's population, a precipitous drop from a decade earlier, proving that the combination of manumissions and slaves escaping to the British greatly impacted the demographics of the township. As former slaves could not return home at war's end (due to reenslavement and the danger of retaliation from vigilante Whigs), most African American Loyalists never returned.

THE AFRICAN AMERICANS WHO STAYED IN MONMOUTH

For the slaves who remained, the war years were hard (as they were for all Monmouthers). Regardless of race, the people of Monmouth County endured dozens of acts of plundering and violence, economic turbulence and the general coarsening of society that occurs amidst civil war. Many slaves freed with Quaker support early in the war years went without support during the later war years. The Shrewsbury Quakers self-critically reported that they had been "unthoughtful of their charge" to support freed African Americans in January 1780. In August 1781, they reported that they were only able to help "some of those already free" due to their own wartime difficulties. In August 1783, the Friends reported with disappointment that the slaves who were freed early in the war by David Cooper and Samuel Allison "are sold back into slavery."

Slaves of white Loyalists who stayed in Monmouth as their masters fled to the British did not receive any special kindness from Whig authorities.

"A Motley Crew at Sandy Hook"

At least ten slaves belonging to four different Loyalist refugees were sold as property to new masters as part of the Loyalist estate confiscations. In other cases, slaves and freedmen became embroiled in lengthy legal processes. In a case ultimately decided before the New Jersey Supreme Court, Caesar Tite, who had been sold by a departing Loyalist early in the war under stipulation that he would be freed on his twenty-first birthday, was held in bondage until age twenty-four by an owner who refused to honor the terms of the original agreement. Tite lost three years of freedom before the courts freed him. Other slaves of white Loyalists, such as those of the Van Mater and Stevenson families, became pawns in legal fights between the kin of their former masters (who claimed them) and the purchasers of the confiscated Loyalist estates. Finally, in a case not settled until 1791, the manumitted family of Cornelius and Hagar Wilson was held seven years beyond their indenture in a dispute between their first slave owner and the man to whom they were sold.

Not all slaves were Loyalists or would-be Loyalists; there are a few examples of slaves showing great compassion and courage in support of Whigs. In June 1778, when Major Thomas Seabrook's home was set afire by British soldiers, an elderly slave of the family heroically extinguished the flames. Dr. John Read recalled being helped by "country people & Negroes" in carrying water to and transporting the suffering soldiers from the battlefield following the Battle of Monmouth. In some cases, Whigs showed a softening in their treatment of slaves during the war years, including allowing fifteen to attend and receive communion at the Presbyterian church at Manalapan for the first time in 1779. By war's end, fifteen free African American families were listed on the county tax rolls as "householders," a slight increase from the 1778–79 tax rolls.

Slavery in New Jersey outlasted the war and was only gradually abolished starting in 1804, making New Jersey the last northern state to end slavery. The harshness of the war became a justification for not abolishing slavery in New Jersey as quickly as in other northern states. An essay printed in the *New Jersey Gazette* in 1780 argued that "at this time when so many parts of the State are laid to waste and rendered desolate by the ravages of war," New Jersey families "depend in great measure on the labor of slaves for their livelihood; it would be unreasonable to deprive them of their only support." The essay also played to fears that freed slaves would "become idle" and "commit plunder and rapine." These arguments persisted into the postwar period.

CONCLUSION

Many (perhaps even most) of the adult male slaves who ran away from Monmouth County during the American Revolution acted as Loyalist irregulars along the military frontier. The empowering and profitable character of this activity was a powerful lure. Among the Loyalist irregulars at Sandy Hook, prospects of success trumped race when determining whether to participate in a raid. White Loyalists were quite willing to serve (at least unofficially) under anyone, including a person of color such as Colonel Tye, if the prospects of success appeared good. The intensity of the actions of the African American Loyalists at Sandy Hook was unique in the northern colonies, but it was not necessarily unique throughout all of the rebelling American colonies. Along other faraway military frontiers, such as the eastern shore of the Chesapeake Bay and the Georgia-Florida border, mixed race groups of "Picaroons" also operated in unofficial military associations with little British support. African American irregulars, whether at Sandy Hook or elsewhere in the rebelling colonies, were self-motivated and were not tools of British military strategists.

It is easy to vilify the irregulars, whose mission it was to rob and plunder the homes and property of Whig civilians and then retreat back across the military frontier to safety behind British lines. However, for the African Americans who fled to the British, there were few attractive options besides raiding. Life behind British lines in New York was depressing and dangerous. Shortages of employment, food and key provisions were constant in New York, and as early as June 1779 there were instances of runaway slaves being kidnapped and sold back into slavery in the Caribbean. So the raider's life at Refugeetown on Sandy Hook, though dangerous, probably offered a greater sense of community, personal autonomy and opportunity for profit than life in New York. Certainly, returning to New Jersey was not an option, since the New Jersey government refused to abolish slavery, and the New Jersey countryside had many vigilante Whigs eager to punish Loyalists. Finally, at least some of the African American partisans were likely fired by the desire to exact revenge on cruel former masters—a base but understandable motivation.

Far from being welcome in the regular British army or the provincial corps of white American Loyalists, most African Americans who did join the British military were relegated to the second-class roles of partisans and porters. In March 1777, General William Howe banned African Americans from serving in regular Loyalist army units, writing to the commanders of the provincial corps that

> *the Commander in Chief, being desirous that the Provincial Corps should be put on the most respectable footing* [with the British army], *has directed that all Negroes, mulattos and other improper persons who have been admitted into the corps, may be immediately discharged—the Inspector General will receive particular orders on the subject to prevent such abuses in the future.*

It appears that only one African American Loyalist served in the New Jersey Volunteers: Thomas Merigold, as the waiter to the paymaster of the corps.

African American Loyalists, shunned from regular service and with little means of support behind British lines, turned to the unsavory business of irregular warfare. The British army, unlike the partially integrated Continental army, was utterly segregated, and African Americans were locked into segregated units with the least attractive roles. Given the lack of opportunity facing the African Americans who sought freedom behind British lines, it is easy to understand why so many former slaves turned to the unsavory business of raiding across the military frontier as their means of support. And given the rough conduct of Monmouth County's Whigs, it is easier to view Monmouth County's African American runaway slaves more as freedom fighters than thugs, though the morass of civil warfare makes such distinctions very subjective.

The success of the Black Brigade in penetrating the military frontier demonstrates the difficulty Whigs faced in defending their land and homesteads. Loyalist irregulars, with the ability to pick the time and place of every strike, had a powerful advantage against the local militia and state troops vainly attempting to patrol Monmouth's extensive coastline. The next chapter examines the spotty record of the Continental soldiers who periodically intervened in the local war in an attempt to provide additional security to Monmouth County's Whigs.

5

"THEY DO RATHER MORE HARM THAN GOOD"

The Continental Army in Monmouth County

ontinental soldiers first entered Monmouth County in June 1776 on a mission to dislodge a detachment of British seamen from Sandy Hook. Two months earlier, sailors from the HMS *Syren* disembarked on the unguarded peninsula and took possession of the Sandy Hook Lighthouse. Sandy Hook's location at the entrance of New York Harbor and the lighthouse gave "the Hook" great strategic importance. The possessor of Sandy Hook controlled access to New York and owned a sheltered anchorage from which its ships could harass shipping throughout New York Harbor and along the New Jersey shoreline.

Lieutenant Colonel Benjamin Tupper commanded a regiment of Massachusetts Continentals that was sent to Sandy Hook to drive off the British. Before dawn on June 21, Tupper's regiment broke camp and marched up the peninsula under cover of the cedar trees that lined Sandy Hook. After coming into a clearing and wheeling their cannon within 250 yards of the lighthouse, Tupper and an officer marched forward to demand the surrender of the British. When the demand was refused, the Continentals fired twenty-one rounds of cannonballs at the lighthouse. The small cannons proved ineffective. Tupper reported finding "the walls so thick as to make no impression," but the Continentals continued to fire on the lighthouse for "about two and a half hours, between the smart fires from men of war on the one side & the Lighthouse on the other." The Continentals were driven off when cannons from the warship HMS *Phoenix* started landing in the clearing "where every man was exposed." Two of Tupper's men were wounded, but none was killed. It is doubtful that any of the defenders, secure inside the lighthouse and surrounding buildings, were hurt.

Tupper retreated two miles from Sandy Hook and considered his options. But he was advised by George Washington to break off the attack because a renewed battle "seems dangerous and not to promise success." Tupper returned to Perth Amboy on the twenty-third. That same day, Lawrence Hartwick, an engineer for the Royal Navy, surveyed Sandy Hook and authored a report on how to improve its defenses, including removing all trees within 525 yards of the lighthouse and fitting the lighthouse for small artillery. The first and best opportunity the Whigs had to force the British off Sandy Hook was lost. Two weeks later, a British soldier at Sandy Hook noted improvements to its defenses and concluded, "We expect it will be attacked again soon, but we are well prepared for them."

The futility of Tupper's assault was partially the result of ineffective artillery. His cannons were too small to seriously threaten the thick walls of the lighthouse. But a second reason for the failure of Tupper's assault is particularly important to this chapter. Tupper's Continentals received no assistance from the residents of Monmouth County, who could have counseled him on the thickness of the lighthouse walls and guided his men to a more advantageous position from which to launch their attack. The inability to get local assistance frustrated Tupper, who wrote to George Washington, "It is a little strainge [sic], I received no help from the Jersies, tho' it was earnestly requested." Tupper's ambivalent reception from the locals foreshadowed several more years of difficult interactions between the Continental army and the residents of Monmouth County.

General George Washington and the commanders of the Continental army were wary about the Continental army intervening in local affairs. They had good reason: first, the Continental army, especially early in the war, was no match for the British army and was not capable of taking on additional responsibilities; second, if Continentals became too involved in local affairs, they could become objects of popular resentment, like the British soldiers under General Gage in Boston. Indeed, it was a belief of General

Washington and most Whig leaders that the Continental army should remain aloof from local affairs, an idea that dovetailed with the prevailing American opinion that standing armies were "engines of tyranny." But due to the extraordinary stresses within Monmouth County, it became one of a few locales where Continental soldiers were frequently sent to intervene in local affairs. This chapter traces their successes and failures.

LOYALIST INSURRECTION AND THE CONTINENTAL RESPONSE

As noted previously, soon after the British fleet anchored at Sandy Hook, on June 29, 1776, large numbers of Monmouthers showed themselves as enemies of the Continental cause, and the county's Loyalists started organizing into armed groups in early July. With much of Monmouth County disaffected and slipping toward insurrection, the New Jersey Convention (the newly named New Jersey Provincial Congress) appealed to the Continental Congress for help, requesting that Continental soldiers intervene and restore order. On July 3, the Continental Congress deliberated, and then its president, John Hancock, wrote to the Pennsylvania Council of Safety:

> *The Congress being informed by an express from the Convention of New Jersey that a number of Tories are embodying themselves in the County of Monmouth, and a considerable number are already encamped in the cedar swamps, and as the power of the militia in that County have marched to New York for the defence of that important place...I apply to you and request that you would immediately send as many troops as your colony can spare to Monmouth County, for the defense and the assistance of the militia and inhabitants.*

On July 4, 1776, as the United States declared itself a nation, the Pennsylvania Council of Safety replied to the Continental Congress's request regarding troops for Monmouth County: "We are extremely sorry to find there are so many men [in Monmouth County] lost to their sense of duty as to embody themselves for the avowed purpose of assisting the enemies of America." It dispatched five hundred Pennsylvania Flying Camps (militia on assignment to the Continental army) to Monmouth under Colonels Samuel Mills and Daniel Broadhead. However, the Pennsylvanians only stayed in

Monmouth County for a few days, camping in Allentown. During this time, a soldier was accidentally shot by his own men, and other disorderly soldiers were banned from buying liquor from the local taverns. Despite the officers' circulating the countersign of "Tory" in their official orders, it appears that the local disaffecteds skillfully feigned loyalty to the new nation. The deception worked, and Samuel Tucker, president of the Convention of New Jersey, requested that the Pennsylvanians march forward to Amboy, noting, "The furor in Monmouth County has already been crushed by our Militia." Subsequent events proved Tucker's assessment grossly incorrect.

East of Allentown, the vulnerability of the Monmouth shoreline was well understood. In March 1776, Lord Stirling mused, "The country is now open to the insult of one [enemy] barge" and proposed posting two companies of Continental soldiers "to guard the coast from Shrewsbury Inlet to the mouth of the Raritan." In July 1776, Pennsylvania Continentals camped across northern Monmouth County, guarding the Raritan Bay shore against British forces on Sandy Hook and Staten Island. On July 18, Colonel Burd arrived at Middletown, and the next day New Jersey governor William Livingston noted the arrival of a body of "Pennsylvania Associators" at another place on the Raritan Bay shore. The buildup of Pennsylvania Continentals was evident along the entire shoreline of northern New Jersey, prompting General Hugh Mercer, on August 10, to boast, "Our whole force, including N. Jersey militia, from Powles Hook to Shrewsbury, amount to eight thousand three hundred." That same month, John Holmes of the Monmouth County committee recorded, "Genl. Mercer has arrived with a Continental Guard at Shrewsbury, who has orders to seize and detain all craft belonging to said shores, and to apprehend suspicious persons."

Despite the Continentals' presence, Monmouth County slid toward anarchy. Two of the three Monmouth County militia regiments became dysfunctional, hampered by disaffection among both officers and the rank and file. Recruiters for the Loyalist New Jersey Volunteers toured the county, and marginally covert Loyalist associations formed in five of the six townships. A profitable contraband trade developed along the county's Atlantic shoreline, funneling the products of Monmouth County farms to an eager British commissary at Sandy Hook. The profits generated by this activity eventually seduced entire neighborhoods into participating.

The Continental soldiers stationed in New Jersey at this time, focused on the campaign in New York, were generally indifferent to the disaffection in

Monmouth County, but they were aware of it. In early November, General Hugh Mercer reported to Congress:

> *The disaffected inhabitants of Monmouth County along the shores of Middletown and Shrewsbury expect daily that the enemy will make a descent on that part of the coast—they are forming associations to join the British on their landing.*

Mercer further reported that the Sussex County militia was on its way to assist the Monmouth militia, but there is no evidence that the Sussex militia ever arrived.

There is only one documented case of Continental soldiers taking action against Monmouth County's Loyalists between August and early November. A party of Virginia Continentals stationed at Amboy, under General Adam Stephen, inadvertently came upon a beached boat at Point Comfort (near the Navesink Highlands). Interrogations of the nine men aboard revealed that the vessel was headed from Staten Island for Long Branch, where the crew would rendezvous with "a parcel of Tories forming a secret encampment in the woods for the purpose of aiding and assisting the British Army." The party's leader, Samuel Wright, and his crew were delivered to the government of New Jersey. The capture of the Loyalist boat successfully broke up Samuel Wright's plan to arm and organize the Loyalists at Long Branch and Shark River but did nothing to hinder any of the other Loyalist associations forming elsewhere in the county. There is no reason to think that Wright's capture was part of an effort to crush the simmering Loyalist insurrection; the capture was accidental. But reports from Mercer and Stephen on disaffection in Monmouth County reached the commander in chief in November—and prompted General Washington to turn to Colonel David Forman, Monmouth County's highest-ranking Continental officer.

Colonel David Forman of Manalapan (near Freehold) raised a regiment of men from Monmouth and Middlesex Counties in May/June 1776 for six months' service in the Continental army and marched off to join the army in New York. By November, Forman's regiment, which had numbered 451 in July, was down to 211 "fit & present" men; the entire regiment's enlistments were set to expire on December 1. Given that the Continental army was about to quit New Jersey and retreat into Pennsylvania, General Washington requested that Colonel Forman leave the Continental army and lead his regiment home to crush the Loyalists. In his orders to Forman, dated November 24, Washington noted that he had "information that there is the danger of an insurrection of Tories in the County of Monmouth." His orders to Forman were broad but explicit:

You are hereby ordered to march, with the regiment under your command, into said County of Monmouth, and on your arrival there, you are authorized to apprehend such persons as appear concerned in any plot or design against the liberty of the United States; and you are further authorized, immediately to attack any body of men whom you may find actually in arms of the purposes aforesaid; and if you should find their numbers superior to your force, you have full authority to call in and take command of such a number of New Jersey Militia as you may judge sufficient.

Forman was also given the power to seize livestock of Monmouthers whose stock was "in danger" of falling into British hands.

Forman's regiment reached Monmouth County on November 25. Within three days, his men arrested nearly one hundred suspected Loyalists and sent them to Philadelphia, where they arrived on December 5 (from there, the Loyalists were sent to Frederick, Maryland). Forman's Continentals seem to have been especially effective in breaking up a Loyalist association in Freehold and Middletown led by the Taylor family (see chapter 3). William Taylor was arrested, and Colonel George Taylor fled to Sandy Hook.

However, Forman became distracted from his campaign against local Loyalists and led his men in a curious attack against Sandy Hook. Forman's defeat was assured when the frigate HMS *Perseus* turned its guns on the attackers. The defeat at the lighthouse seems to have had important ramifications. First, it demoralized the men of Forman's regiment, making them less willing stay beyond December 1. Second, the campaign against the Sandy Hook Lighthouse prevented Forman's regiment from finishing the job it had started: crushing the local insurrection. Forman never went against the budding Loyalist associations in Shrewsbury and Upper Freehold or the widely disaffected lower shore townships of Dover and Stafford.

The dissolution of Forman's regiment, coupled with the march of the British army through New Jersey in early December, brought the Loyalists into the open. Samuel Mount of the Monmouth militia recorded that on December 3, "Monmouth was overrun by the British and Refugees & the militia were compelled to lay down their arms." Forman's regiment offered no resistance. One of Forman's men, William Anderson, referred to this as "the Ascendancy of the Tories" and conceded that the men of his regiment "laid down their arms." Mount's and Anderson's accounts are corroborated in other records.

By mid-December, the Continental cause was at its lowest point. Washington's shrinking and shivering Continental army was in Pennsylvania, and British troops were masters of New Jersey. The situation was even worse for supporters of the Continental cause in Monmouth County. A proclamation issued by General William Howe on November 30, 1776, promised protection to New Jersey residents who would sign an oath of loyalty to the king. In Monmouth County, hundreds took advantage of the offer. Both Forman's regiment and the Whig militia ceased to exist. Monmouth County was under Loyalist control without a single British soldier in the county (excluding Sandy Hook).

The situation in Monmouth County at the close of 1776 must be at least partially attributed to the ineffective Continentals who were stationed in Monmouth County in the summer and fall of that year. In July, a regiment of Pennsylvania Continentals was sent to Monmouth County to subdue the Loyalists, but it stayed only two days. Throughout the fall, Continental soldiers made frequent patrols of the Raritan Bay shore but turned a blind eye to local events. Of greater importance, the regiment of Monmouth County Continentals under Colonel David Forman never completed its job of breaking up the Loyalist associations.

However, the indifference of the Continental army to events in Monmouth County reversed after the Battle of Trenton on Christmas. Again, the course of the larger war set the tone, as the British retreat following the Battle of Trenton opened the county up to Continental army penetration. By December 30, detachments of Pennsylvania and Delaware Continentals were camped at Allentown, the center of Loyalist activities in western Monmouth County. (Allentown hosted so many Continentals that the officers from the Delaware and Pennsylvania detachments nearly came to blows over quartering arrangements.) Five Loyalists were arrested by the Continentals before the Pennsylvania detachment marched east to engage the main body of Loyalists mustered at Freehold.

On January 2, 1777, a column of 120 Pennsylvania Continentals, under Lieutenant Colonel Francis Gurney, engaged a body of 200 Loyalists at Freehold. Forewarned, the Loyalists, under Colonel John Morris, retreated with their baggage toward Middletown, a move probably calculated to place the clash with the Continentals in a neighborhood where the Loyalist recruits might receive British support. But the retreat went slowly, and the Continentals caught up with the Loyalists only a mile and a half east of Freehold. Adam Hubley, a Pennsylvania officer, recorded the engagement:

> *We immediately push'd after them, when they made a halt, we came up, about a quarter of an hour before night, when we engaged them, and they stood us about eight minutes, a very heavy fire was kept up between us for that time. The enemy at last gave way, and retreated very precipitously, at this time it was quite dark, and we could not see what loss the enemy sustained, but our side we had none killed.*

By the next morning, the Continentals had found four dead bodies in the snow and taken twenty-three prisoners, seven wagonloads of supplies and twelve horses. A few days later, Captain Smith captured twenty-two more Loyalists, probably remnants of the same group.

Gurney's Continentals maintained a strong presence in Monmouth County after the battle. They continued east from Freehold and spent several weeks combing the county for Loyalists and supplies that had been stockpiled for the British army. Nathaniel Scudder accompanied Gurney, noting with satisfaction that he "marched with the detachment and continued with them until the enemy was entirely dispersed & their supplies at Middletown seized." Similar actions took place at Shrewsbury, where a second Continental detachment set up camp. On January 15, the *Pennsylvania Journal and Weekly Advertiser* noted that the Continentals were in Shrewsbury, "where they took a large quantity of cloth and other stores, collected by a sett [*sic*] of Tories." The staying power of the Continentals was put to the test at least once. On January 9, General Israel Putnam wrote that "the Tories of Monmouth are again in arms, Col. Gurney marched today to suppress them." The Pennsylvanians dispersed all organized opposition.

By late January 1777, Monmouth County was effectively occupied by the Continental army and a reforming local militia. Instead of leaving after defeating the assembled Loyalists at Freehold, the Continentals spent the entire month seizing the war materials and suspected Loyalists. Caesar Rodney, at Trenton, observed that "Coll. Gurney, who was sent by Genl. Putnam with five hundred men into Monmouth, has taken a very large quantity of stores," estimating that Gurney had sent back forty wagonloads of provisions, including "a great quantity of cloathes [*sic*] and other English goods." With satisfaction, General Israel Putnam reported his decision to leave Gurney's men in Monmouth County:

> *The Colonel supposes that about one hundred wagon loads* [are] *still remaining, he discovers more daily—they chiefly consist of rum, wine, pork and broad cloth—I have thought it best to let Colonel Gurney stay down where he is, until the militia are well-embodied.*

The fervor with which the Pennsylvanians confiscated the goods of Monmouthers did not go without incident. Gurney's men were accused of plundering the cargo of a Massachusetts ship beached at Long Branch and of driving off one of Daniel Hendrickson's (a colonel in the Monmouth militia) wagons. However, these small controversies do not obscure the overall success of the campaign.

By early February 1777, Loyalist associations in Monmouth County were defeated, prompting General Putnam to conclude, "The affairs in Monmouth wear a favorable aspect. The people of that County will again return to their duties." The exception were the two secluded shore townships (Dover and Stafford) where Gurney's men never marched, though an additional party of Pennsylvania soldiers was sent to the Pennsylvania Saltworks at Toms River to protect them. The most strident Loyalists were either arrested or in exile, mostly the latter. While disaffection remained a problem in Monmouth County throughout the war, the organized Loyalist insurrections were over. On February 5, when the Pennsylvanians left Monmouth County, Nathaniel Scudder publicly thanked Lieutenant Colonel Gurney and Major John Davis of Cumberland County (whose militia supported the Pennsylvanians): "Your detachments have rescued the county from the tyranny of the Tories."

David Forman as Military and Political Commander

With the Loyalists defeated and dispersed, Monmouth's Whigs were faced with two formidable tasks: 1) revitalizing the county militia and keeping the disaffected in check and 2) defending the county's long and vulnerable coastline from British and Loyalist raiders based on Sandy Hook and Staten Island. To accomplish this, the government of New Jersey and General Washington took the exceptional step of consolidating power in the hands of David Forman. By March, Forman was one of three brigadier generals of the New Jersey Militia (with jurisdiction over Monmouth, Middlesex and Burlington Counties) and also colonel of an additional regiment of the Continental army (recruiting men from Monmouth County into the Continental army to provide local defense outside of usual Continental army assignments).

Under the leadership of Forman and Nathaniel Scudder, the first regiment of the Monmouth militia mustered again on February 1, 1777, while the Pennsylvanians were still in the county. But raising an effective militia in the more disaffected townships was difficult. The disaffection of the Dover militia, for example, caused Thomas Savadge, a Pennsylvanian at Toms River, to write on February 10:

> *The militia of this part of the country are by no means calculated for the defense thereof; for more than half of them are Tories, and the rest but little better. I am of the opinion that if this part of the country is to be defended it must be by Continental troops, who know their duty, or by Militia from another State.*

But David Forman was convinced that the best way to keep the disaffecteds in their place was to coerce universal militia service (legally mandated but not enforced). The idea of rearming and organizing people who, a few weeks earlier, had supported the Loyalist ascendancy was controversial. George Washington was initially against Forman's plan, writing, "I fear he has not the strength for it & as to their Militia, if they [the disaffected] do turn out, they will be of more hurt than good."

Meanwhile, Forman continued to raise men for his new Continental regiment. Local recruiting went badly (only one of eight companies reached even half strength), forcing Forman to recruit men from Maryland and Delaware. By May, Forman's regiment still had fewer than one hundred men, at least in part because other Continental army recruiters were offering greater recruiting inducements. In frustration, Forman petitioned the Continental Congress, asking to be "put on a respectable footing" with other recruiters. Never one to mince words, Forman claimed that he was "under such restrictions as amounting, in all its consequences, to an entire prohibition [on recruiting]." Forman grew so desperate for men that he even recruited Monmouth Loyalists jailed in Philadelphia, an effort that yielded modest results: seven new recruits.

Forman's recruiting problems were small in comparison to the controversies stemming from his conduct. Forman had invested heavily in the Union Saltworks at Manasquan, but these grand works had to be protected. Forman made sure his works were secure, stationing a company of soldiers at his still incomplete works. While there, the soldiers were put to work as laborers. Not only were Forman's soldiers working for a private enterprise he co-owned, but they were also harvesting wood from the land of Trevor Newland, a former magistrate under the royal government and a British army officer during the Seven Years' War. Newland lodged a complaint with the New Jersey Council of Safety, which concluded that Forman's Continentals at the Union Saltworks "have not been of any use to the publick; but have been employed to promote the private interest of individuals." Despite the rebuke, the government of New Jersey took no immediate action against Forman. The conflict of interest was further complicated when Forman, in his other capacity as general of the Monmouth militia, ordered the Dover militia away from the saltworks of his principal competitor, Thomas Savadge. On February 15, Savadge wrote a desperate appeal to the Pennsylvania government for protection because "Coll. Furman [*sic*] has ordered the militia here to march from this place to Freehold."

On March 20, Forman proceeded with plans for a general militia muster for Monmouth, Middlesex and Burlington Counties, but Governor William Livingston was skeptical. At Forman's request, George Washington wrote to Livingston in support of Forman's plan for a general muster and campaign against the disaffected. In his letter, Washington reversed his previous skepticism about Forman's plan:

> It will not only distinguish the well-affected from the ill, but it will prevent the Tories from poisoning the minds of the People. Coll. Forman further informs me that many of the people who have absconded have left behind them stocks of horses, cattle and grain, which will not only be lost to the owners but also to the publick if some mode is not fallen upon to secure them.

Governor Livingston was less than enthusiastic about Forman's plan. On April 4, Livingston wrote to Washington that the Burlington and Middlesex militias were "exceedingly dilatory in their motions" and that those militias "will probably be of as much service at home as they can be elsewhere." Indeed, the governor was right. On April 13, a desperate Forman wrote to General Israel Putnam for assistance:

A party of British troops were discovered making from the Hook to Middletown; I shall immediately put myself in their way and attempt to attack them—at present I am very weak here, my numbers do not exceed 160 rank and file.

The invading party was actually composed of Loyalists. They moved past Middletown, burned down the Presbyterian meetinghouse near Middletown Point and captured Reverend Charles McKnight, one of the county's leading Whigs. There is no evidence that Forman was able to offer any resistance, although he did report dispersing a different body of Loyalists on April 14.

By spring, Forman's grand scheme for the defense of Monmouth County—a full regiment of Continental soldiers backed by a strong county militia and detachments from neighboring counties—was in shambles. A letter to Forman from Nathaniel Scudder acknowledged the "weakness of your posts and the distress of our friends in consequence of the depredations of the enemy." Scudder, a member of the New Jersey Council of Safety, cautioned that Forman not rely on militia officers who had signed British loyalty oaths during the Loyalist ascendancy and had not signed Continental loyalty oaths afterward. Despite Forman's weakness, General Washington declined Forman's appeals for six cannons to use for a proposed fortification on the Navesink Highlands, to defend against incursions from Sandy Hook. Without the cannons, Forman appears to have given up attempting to defend eastern Monmouth County. A Loyalist newspaper in New York City boasted in June:

We hear that Mr. Forman, with about 400 of the Rebel Army, has abandoned Shrewsbury, and is gone to Middletown, about 12 miles distant. Many of the Committeemen and other hot people have followed Mr. Forman's example, being apprehensive of a visit.

Meanwhile, the condition of Forman's additional regiment deteriorated. In August, Forman wrote to Colonel Trumbull that "the troops on this station are very sickly," which was understandable given the heat and hard labor they were enduring at the saltworks. The continued controversy surrounding Forman's stationing of men at his own saltworks forced George Washington to take action (and may have caused Congress to decline Forman's petition to raise a new one-hundred-man guard for the saltworks). Washington transferred command of Forman's regiment to Colonel Israel Shreve of

Burlington County "to avoid the imputation of partiality and remove the cause of censure." In early 1778, Forman's additional regiment was removed from Monmouth County and merged into the main body of the Continental army. Forman no longer commanded any men, not even in his own county (though he continued to hold the rank of colonel in the Continental army).

Despite the setbacks at the end of 1777, David Forman had changed the nature of the local war in Monmouth County. In the more densely inhabited northern parts of Monmouth County, he had successfully reconstituted the Monmouth County militia and struck fear into the disaffecteds, who were now muted in their opposition to the Whig government. Forman's accomplishments were, however, achieved at a tremendous cost. Through his harsh tactics, Forman drove dozens of Monmouth County's disaffected citizens across British lines, where many became embittered Loyalists. This fact is confirmed by the swelled muster rolls of the Loyalist New Jersey Volunteers. More Monmouthers went into the volunteers in the first six months of 1777 than in all other months of the war combined.

Exiled, separated from their families and often impoverished, these so-called refugees, sheltered and armed by the British army on Sandy Hook and Staten Island, proved a much more serious problem than the Loyalist associations within the county in 1776. After 1777, the Revolution in Monmouth County changed from a limited war between local factions, bound by proximity to behave with some civility, to a vindictive irregular war fought across enemy lines.

Raid Warfare and the Continental Response

Irregular warfare increased in 1778. In early April, with Forman's Continentals removed, a British/Loyalist raiding party razed his saltworks at Manasquan without opposition. Appeals were quickly made to George Washington for Continental troops to defend the exposed New Jersey shoreline. On April 14, 1778, Washington outlined his opinion regarding the perceived versus real value of Continental troops in protecting the exposed shoreline:

> *A few hundred Continental troops quiet the minds and give satisfaction to the people of the country; but considered in the true light, they do rather more harm than good. They draw over the attention of the enemy, and being*

not able to resist them, are obliged to fly and leave the country at the mercy of the foe. But as I said before, the people do not view things in the same light, and therefore they must be indulged, tho' to their detriment.

However, it is not clear which troops, if any, Washington used to "indulge" the people of Monmouth County; there is no record of Continental troops in Monmouth County in the first half of 1778. It was not until June 25 that Continental troops again entered Monmouth County, and that was in pursuit of General Henry Clinton's British army in the days leading up to the Battle of Monmouth. On June 28, 1778, the two armies fought at the Battle of Monmouth, one of the largest battles of the war, near Freehold, yet the main bodies of both armies left the county within a week.

Following the Battle of Monmouth, Sandy Hook was fortified with twenty-five hundred British soldiers to protect the peninsula against an expected attack from a French fleet that had recently arrived in American waters. The need to provision these men spiked the simmering illegal trade between Sandy Hook and the disaffecteds of Monmouth County to new heights and left Monmouth County vulnerable to invasion. This prompted Colonel Asher Holmes, commanding the county's militia, to appeal to Governor Livingston on August 4:

The inhabitants of the lower part of the County are much exposed…Forces are not sufficient to oppose the enemy in case they should come, which I have the greatest reason to believe they will, as it is in their power at any time… and not one Continental soldier near for our defense. [I] would therefore request that part of Gen Maxwell's brigade be sent in the County.

Within a few weeks, Major Richard Howell and a party of thirty Continentals were stationed at Black Point, near the mouth of the Shrewsbury River. Howell's mission was to monitor the movements of the British fleet at Sandy Hook and disrupt the burgeoning London trade that was flourishing between the residents of Shrewsbury and Sandy Hook. However, there is reason to believe that Howell's men became involved in the London trade. On October 21, Washington wrote to Lord Stirling (Howell's senior commander), noting that there had been "some instances of commerce between the inhabitants [of Monmouth County] and the enemy, which may have been tolerated" by Howell's men. Washington ordered Stirling to investigate, writing, "If you discover any improper connivance on the part of the officers at Shrewsbury, you will take proper measures not only to prevent it in the future, but to punish it in the past."

That same month, a large amphibious force, composed of over one thousand British and Loyalists, landed near Little Egg Harbor and razed the village of Chestnut Neck, New Jersey's largest privateer base. A Continental artillery regiment under Colonel Thomas Proctor was dispatched to check the raiders, as was the newly mustered Continental Legion under Kasimir Pulaski, which set up camp on Osborn's Island at the southern tip of Monmouth County. The Third Regiment of the Monmouth militia, under Colonel Samuel Forman, and militia regiments from Burlington and Gloucester Counties also mustered (since the invaders had landed at the junction of all three counties). However, coordination among the American forces was never established and—though collectively formidable—the American forces did little but shadow the British/Loyalist parties as they laid waste to several homes, saltworks and ships in the Mullica River and at Little Egg Harbor.

Of the American units, it seems that Count Pulaski's Legion (at least based on his own letters) was the most vigilant in attempting to check the British threat. However, the camp he established on Osborn's Island was dangerously close to the British ships. On the night of October 15, Pulaski's corps was attacked by a party of Loyalists under Captain Patrick Ferguson. Dozens of sleeping Continentals were slaughtered. The brutality of the action surprised even General Sir Henry Clinton, who later required Ferguson to account for the merciless attack. In the days that followed, Pulaski followed the British—who had returned to their boats in safety—north into Monmouth County "for fear that they [the British] should burn as they go on." On his march through Barnegat and the other villages of lower Monmouth County, the locals earned the scorn of Pulaski. He claimed, "We are betrayed on all sides" by locals who "make a sport" of sniping at his men.

With Pulaski's discouraging letters in mind, Washington quickly pulled the detachments under Pulaski, Proctor and Howell from Monmouth County. Two months later, on December 14, Governor Livingston again asked for Continentals to protect Monmouth County, suggesting, "Perhaps about 400 Continental troops stationed in that county at Middletown Point, the other at Middletown, and the third at Shrewsberry [sic] might be a sufficient guard." But Washington diplomatically refused: "I have already distributed largely for the security of the State, and the security of the inhabitants has been of particular consideration, but it is impossible to include every place." But it was not long before Washington changed his mind.

The London trade between Monmouth County and the British base at Sandy Hook was a growing concern of Washington's. On January 8, 1779, Washington wrote, "I have received such repeated information of the trade that is carried on between Monmouth and New York, that I find it an absolute necessity of sending down a party to that quarter to put a stop to that intercourse." A few days later, he ordered Colonel Caleb North's regiment of Pennsylvania Continentals to Monmouth County, where they positioned themselves across northern Shrewsbury Township, "one company at Red Bank, one at Shrewsbury, two at Eatontown, one at the Falls [Tinton Falls]." Washington cautioned North regarding the locals: "You will be a troublesome neighbor to some of them." There is little evidence that North's troops were very helpful while in Monmouth County (though they did prevent the capture of a stranded Whig ship), and they were notably unruly. They robbed Essek Hartshorne, a prominent citizen, and one of the Continental companies mutinied. In addition, the local leaders at Middletown Point and Toms River complained that North's men were not stationed to appropriately defend their villages. Some of North's men deserted or supported the London trade while in Monmouth County. Washington confided to Governor Livingston that Loyalist agents "have been active in corrupting our men."

That March, Washington and Livingston discussed constructing of a beacon warning system to alert Continental troops near Shrewsbury of any attempt by the British to cut them off by landing to the west. The beacons were constructed later that year. Caleb North's Pennsylvania Continentals were replaced by a regiment of Maryland Continentals under Colonel Mordecai Gist. But Gist's men also had a difficult time in Monmouth County. Stationed too far from the Continental commissary, they had to purchase food and clothing at usurious rates from disaffected Monmouthers. The situation prompted Gist to write an angry petition to the Continental Congress, claiming that:

We have the mortification to see the troops of every State provided with cloathing [sic] and other necessaries at reasonable and moderate prices, whilst we alone have been obliged to purchase from private stores every necessity at the most exorbitant rates.

Gist's petition foreshadowed even greater problems for his detachment. On April 3, 1779, a detachment of Gist's Continentals mutinied near

Middletown, and the colonel requested the assistance of the Monmouth militia to put down the mutiny. A letter from Colonel Daniel Hendrickson to Captain Barnes Smock and Colonel Asher Holmes of the Monmouth militia discussed the situation:

> *Coll. Gist has requested of me to let Coll. Holmes know that that he stands in need of assistance of the militia in order to bring his men to order, that one company hath mutiny'd at Middletown and are determined to go off to the enemy if not prevented, and desires that Coll. Holmes would assist him with about fifty militia tomorrow at Middletown.*

It appears that Gist's regiment was withdrawn from Monmouth County shortly after the mutiny.

Gist's regiment was replaced by Colonel Benjamin Ford's Virginia Continentals, headquartered at Tinton Falls. Almost immediately, Ford's men alienated the residents of the surrounding villages. The ill-disciplined guard stationed in the village of Shrewsbury attempted to dislodge the iron crown (a symbol of the British monarchy) from the local Anglican church by firing musket balls into the church steeple. Unable to dislodge the crown, they then set fire to the church (the fire was quickly extinguished by locals). Soon after, a party of five Loyalist raiders successfully ambushed and captured the twelve-man guard at Shrewsbury, probably with the complicity of disaffected inhabitants.

By April 22, Washington was convinced it was time to pull Ford's men out of Monmouth County, writing to Governor Livingston:

> *You will perceive that I mean to withdraw the Monmouth detachment; an additional motive for it is that the enemy appear to have a number of active emissaries in the part of the country, who have been very successful in corrupting our men. An alarming spirit of mutiny and desertion has shown itself on several occasions and there is no saying how far the infection might spread.*

Meanwhile, Ford's Continentals were less than vigilant in their duty of patrolling the shoreline for raiding parties. Captain William Beatty wrote about his time in Shrewsbury Township as if it were a vacation: "I went in a detachment to Shrewsbury in Monmouth County, here we continued very peaceable, spending our spare time with a number of fine ladies in this neighbourhood." The relaxed nature of Beatty's service contrasts sharply to the hard duty that he and his comrades were sent to perform.

However, before they could be pulled out of Monmouth County, Ford's regiment experienced profound humiliation. On April 25, a two-pronged attack was launched into Monmouth County by approximately eight hundred British and Loyalists intent on capturing Ford's regiment, which, according to Sir Henry Clinton, "lay in an exposed position at Shrewsbury and Middletown." The first party of raiders, comprising Loyalists and led by the energetic Patrick Ferguson, landed along the Shrewsbury River and headed straight for Tinton Falls, where they had orders to engage Ford's Continentals. Meanwhile, the second party of raiders, mostly British regulars commanded by Colonel West Hyde, landed on the Raritan Bay shore and marched south hoping to cut off the Continentals from the west. However, the plans of the raiders were not realized because of Colonel Ford's temerity. Upon the first report of the landing of troops at Shrewsbury, Ford ordered his entire regiment to retreat to Colts Neck (near Freehold), never engaging the raiders and leaving the badly outnumbered Monmouth militia to offer what little resistance it could. In ordering this precipitous retreat, Ford sacrificed his own twenty-two-man scout party at Shrewsbury, under Captain Samuel Bell.

When Ferguson's raiders arrived at Tinton Falls, only to find that Ford's men had retreated hours earlier, the raiders razed the village. William Smith, the Loyalist attorney general of New York, wrote that Ferguson's party "took between 20 and 30 prisoners, and burnt a mill and two or three houses." Smith's appraisal, however, reveals only a fraction of the plundering that occurred at Tinton Falls. Benjamin White, a storekeeper at Tinton Falls, vividly recalled the conduct of the raiders:

> So enraged that they had lost their prey, they set fire to the houses and burned and plundered many of them on their return. I hid most of our dry goods but they broke open the store, robbed us of what they could, filled their canteens with spirits and let the rest run to waste. They had my mare out and [were] going off with her, and while I was tussling with the soldiers, others were plundering my house; the guns left by our troops were broken across the fence. They seemed like wild or mad men.

Ford's Continentals returned to Tinton Falls the next day. In the aftermath of the raid, the residents of Tinton Falls were understandably angry with the Continentals. Robert Morris, the chief justice of New Jersey, was dispatched to the area and reported that the raiders had "committed the most wanton acts of destruction I ever beheld." He also reported, "Coll. Ford is censured by some of the inhabitants for his conduct." No doubt, Morris was understating the ill feelings, especially from the abandoned Monmouth militia, which responded heroically during the raid by harassing both raiding parties throughout the day.

Washington had hoped to pull Ford's regiment out of Monmouth County even before the disastrous raid, but Ford's regiment remained at Tinton Falls until the end of May. During that time, they did little, not even intervening in raids launched against areas in proximity to Tinton Falls. It remains a mystery exactly why Ford's regiment continued in Monmouth County so long. Perhaps Washington, though deeply cynical about the value of the Continentals in guarding against incursions, believed some Continental presence was, nevertheless, required. On April 28, while reporting to the Continental Congress, Washington revealed his greatest fear about eastern Monmouth County. He warned that the raid might be the first step in a larger British plan:

> They [the British] *may have something more permanent in view—the establishment of a post in that part of the country for the purpose of acquiring greater supplies from that quarter, encouraging the disaffected and obtaining recruits.*

So real was the threat to Washington that he went against his instincts and left Ford's Continentals in Monmouth County for a full month after their ineffectiveness had been proven.

The poor records of the Continentals under North, Gist and Ford (and for that matter Howell and Pulaski before them) in Monmouth County was the embodiment of Washington's fears, as stated in his letter to Livingston a year earlier. His Continental troops had, in fact, done "rather more harm than good." Not only were they ineffective at preventing raids, but they also encouraged them by serving as an attractive target. The rowdy rank and file was involved in numerous disorders, including illicit trading, destruction of private property, mutinies and desertions. Though the war continued for three more years in Monmouth County, and the ferocity of the Loyalist raids in 1780 and 1781 equaled the raids of 1779, Washington never again stationed troops in eastern Monmouth County. Events had proven his gloomy prediction correct.

HENRY "LIGHT HORSE HARRY" LEE IN MONMOUTH COUNTY

When Benjamin Ford's demoralized troops left Monmouth County at the end of May 1779, it was supposed to be the last time that Continental troops were stationed in Monmouth County. However, the Revolutionary War itself was only half over, and it became necessary for Continental soldiers to return. Each winter, officers from the Quartermaster Department toured Monmouth County, purchasing grain and stock for the army in winter quarters. In addition, Continental officers from Monmouth County, such as Major John Burrowes, were periodically active on the local scene. Yet these were individuals without substantial commands. Large bodies of Continental troops were not assigned for long periods in Monmouth County after Ford's departure, with the exception of the elite dragoons of Henry "Light Horse Harry" Lee.

Lee's regiment was sent into Monmouth County three times, in September 1779 and again in July and November 1780, for the purpose of rendezvousing with anticipated French fleets. In Monmouth County, Lee's men had little formal responsibility; only a small number of men were needed to scout the shoreline at any given time. Lee did not station his men near the shore but sent scouts out intermittently to search the shore for the French ships. He maintained his headquarters at Freehold, fifteen miles inland. The decision to set up camp at Freehold was in keeping with Washington's orders. Washington stated that Lee should set up headquarters in a secure place "without making yourself liable to a surprise." Choosing headquarters inland in a Whig neighborhood had the effect of providing Lee's men with security and limiting their contact with the disaffected inhabitants along the shore.

Free from the miserable task of guarding the shoreline, Lee's men were capable of assisting the Whigs of Monmouth County. During their time of duty in Monmouth County, Lee's men performed several acts that endeared them to local Whigs. On September 23, a party of Lee's men under Sergeant John Cusak worked in concert with a few Monmouthers in hunting down Lewis Fenton, the notorious Pine Robber. In January 1780, Lee's men launched two successful raids against the British base at Sandy Hook. In the first action, they captured several Loyalists and a large quantity of counterfeit Continental currency, and in the second action they burned two ships docked at Horseshoe Bay, halfway up the Sandy Hook Peninsula. While on his second tour of duty in Monmouth, in July 1780, Lee's men worked with David Forman and other Monmouth Whigs in rounding up horses and livestock belonging to disaffected Monmouthers. Lee also issued passports to Monmouthers to visit imprisoned relatives in New York and paid for his own forage without going through the Quartermaster Department, moves that earned him rebukes from Judge David Imlay and Quartermaster Agent David Rhea but probably also earned him the friendship of Monmouthers. Lee even praised the people of Monmouth County in a letter to Washington: "I found the country to which I was sent very patriotic & the magistrates anxious to give every aid to the Army."

Washington, no doubt relieved that Lee's mission had not turned into a disaster, was willing to send more Continental troops into Monmouth County one more time. He ordered Colonel Charles Armand's regiment (the successor of Pulaski's corps) to establish their winter quarters in Monmouth "and aided by a Party of Lee's Light Dragoons, endeavour [sic] to stop the communication with New-York from that quarter." It is unclear how successful this mission was, but there is evidence that Armand's Continentals suffered from desertions, probably the result of being stationed close to the British and in a disaffected neighborhood. On February 14, 1780, the Loyalist attorney general, William Smith of New York, interrogated Robert Abraham, a deserter from Armand's Continentals. Abraham noted the vulnerable position of his former regiment, telling Smith that "100 men might bring off the whole 300 in Monmouth; they [his former regiment] have 40 horse there but keep only 16 horse shodd [sic], to prevent desertions." Armand did not stay much longer.

The successful record of Lee's dragoons while in Monmouth County contrasts sharply with the records of the Continentals who preceded them. This raises the question: why were Lee's men successful while other Continentals were so unsuccessful? No doubt, the answer has something to do with the exceptional nature of Lee's dragoons, who were better paid and supplied than other Continental units. Lee's exceptional abilities as a commander certainly played a role, too. But another reason for the success of Lee's men was the limited nature of their mission, allowing them to assist the locals in prosecuting the local war rather than being relied upon to prosecute the local war themselves. The irony of the success of Lee's dragoons was that in being asked to do less, they were able to do more.

———

When Lee's dragoons departed Monmouth County for the final time, it was the last time that a significant detachment of Continental soldiers camped there. Though the irregular warfare continued through 1782, apparently Washington and other Whig leaders decided that the safety of Whigs in Monmouth County could not be guaranteed by Continental troops, so there was no compelling reason to put the troops at risk. However, Monmouthers continued to suffer, and the government of New Jersey continued to request help from the Continental army.

In January 1782, Pine Robber gangs reportedly numbering over one hundred men, under the command of the infamous John Bacon and the mysterious "Davenport," menaced the Monmouth shoreline from Manasquan to Barnegat. They defeated militia detachments and privateer vessels. The Pine Robbers posed the most serious threat to lower Monmouth County since Ferguson's campaign in 1778. After receiving a flurry of letters and petitions from the residents of Toms River and the other shore villages, Governor William Livingston wrote to Washington requesting troops to guard the shore. On January 12, 1782, Washington responded somewhat angrily to Livingston's request, denying it on three grounds. First, the commander in chief claimed that the strength of the Loyalists was exaggerated and that Livingston's report was not "well grounded." Second, Washington argued that New Jersey would continue to suffer from Loyalist partisans within its borders until London trading (which co-opted locals into supporting the Loyalists) became a capital offense. However, it was Washington's third argument that was probably his primary motive for denying Livingston's request. Plainly stated, Washington wrote, "No force which I could spare would prevent it [Pine Robber activity], as they would, if kept out of one inlet, use another for their purposes." Protecting the long and exposed shoreline was too difficult a job for a regiment of Continentals.

CONCLUSION

As stated in the beginning of this chapter, George Washington and other leaders of the fledgling United States were never comfortable with Continental soldiers intervening in domestic affairs. Each state, through its principal military instrument, the militia, was responsible for policing and subduing its own disaffected population, and the Continental army was responsible for combating foreign enemies (i.e., the British). This created a dichotomy of roles for the Continental army and the state militias, but the realities of war made this dichotomy impracticable along the military frontier, and Continental soldiers had to intervene in particularly distressed localities such as Monmouth County.

After demonstrating indifference in 1776, Continental soldiers were extremely successful in the early months of 1777 in breaking up the overt Loyalist associations and driving the county's armed and organized Loyalists behind British lines. Conversely, Continental soldiers were totally incapable, during the middle years of the war, of defending the Monmouth shore against Loyalist irregulars or curbing the London trade. In fact, the difficult assignments in Monmouth County weakened the Continentals through mutinies, desertions, captures and demoralizing raids. From 1781 onward, the Whigs of Monmouth County were on their own to defend themselves, even though it was well understood that they were not able to effectively patrol the shorelines or police the disaffected. Frustrated by their vulnerability and disappointed by the lack of assistance from the Continental and state governments, some Monmouth County Whigs were driven toward tactics as lawless and violent as those of their enemies. The next chapter examines the rise of the infamous vigilante organization, the Association for Retaliation.

This chapter is based on a paper presented at a symposium at Morristown National Historical Park in 1995, though it has been considerably modified and updated.

6

"A Combination to Trample All Law Underfoot"

Monmouth County's Retaliators

As the war began, James and Rhoda Pew lived modestly on an eighteen-acre farm near the Raritan Bay. Like many people in that part of the county, the Pews were disaffected and likely participated in the London trade. Their disaffection was eventually uncovered, and they were indicted for misdemeanor (probably London trading) in June 1778. James Pew fled behind British lines and joined a ship in the service of the British quartermaster, thereby formalizing his role in London trading. Rhoda Pew left for New York soon after. The family estate was "inquisitioned for forfeiture," meaning the state declared it eligible for confiscation and sale at public auction.

Later that year, James Pew returned home to visit family and conduct illegal trade (James's father and brothers remained in Monmouth). On November 10, 1778, he was discovered, captured and jailed in Freehold. Five days later, while in the cellar jail of the county courthouse, James Pew was shot at close range by the guard, James Tilley. Rhoda Pew told British authorities that her husband "was put to death by the sentry, who discharged his musket through wicket hole [in the prison door] and shot the prisoner as he was sitting on a bench before the fire; he then took another musket and shot him a second time through the body."

James Tilley was a man of modest standing (he did not own land) and without many family connections in Monmouth County. Tilley's motivation for murdering Pew is unknown, but curiously, Tilley never stood trial. He was brought before an extralegal tribunal, rather than a civil court, and acquitted. A year earlier, Colonel David Forman had convened a similar extralegal tribunal to consider the fate of a captured Loyalist, Stephen Edwards, and then summarily hanged him before the governor could even consider a pardon (pardons were common for capital convictions early in the war). It appears that Monmouth's more radical Whig leaders were deliberately subverting the courts to cover up brutal actions taken in the name of more vigorously prosecuting the war against Loyalists.

At least initially, Pew's murder and the strange extralegal maneuverings afterward aroused no outcry, not even from the Loyalist community in New York. It was not until 1782, when the Loyalist refugees in New York were desperate to prove the gross misconduct of Monmouth's vigilante Whigs, that the details of Pew's murder were documented. The murder of Pew was one of a score of brutal actions compiled in a report of "Acts of Cruelty and Barbarity" committed by the vigilante Whigs of Monmouth County. Tilley left Monmouth County (he does not appear in the 1779 tax rolls or any local document afterward), probably moving inland to avoid Loyalist reprisal or to escape the lingering scandal associated with his name. But the radical Whigs who abetted Tilley in late 1778 were just beginning their five-year embrace of extralegal retaliation.

BACKGROUND AND PRECEDENTS FOR RETALIATION

The murders of the Loyalists Edwards and Pew had important repercussions in Monmouth County. First, they embittered revenge-minded Loyalists. Second, and especially important to this chapter, because neither incident drew censure from the New Jersey government, they set the stage for more brazen actions. Monmouth's vigilantes even found support for their retaliatory acts in the resolves of the Continental Congress. On October 30, 1778, Congress threatened to practice eye-for-an-eye retaliation against the British following the October 15 massacre of Pulaski's Legion on Osborn's Island (as discussed in the previous chapter).

In 1779, Loyalist raids increased in frequency and ferocity. A pair of devastating raids caused the evacuation of Tinton Falls, the only Whig stronghold near Sandy Hook, and most militia officers in Shrewsbury Township were either captured or forced to move inland for safety. Large tracts of sparsely inhabited pinelands inside the county became staging grounds for Pine Robbers and pushed the war within Monmouth County to a more chilling level. For many Monmouth Whigs, the extraordinary danger made eye-for-an-eye retaliation (outside the guidance of the state government or any legitimate authority) an attractive response.

Driven to desperation, Monmouth Whigs first sought permission to punish their enemies through retaliation on May 25, 1779. They petitioned the New Jersey legislature, "setting forth that many of the inhabitants of sd. County have been plundered and deprived of their property by some of the fugitives who have joined the enemy, and praying a reimbursement out of the fugitives' estates." The petition ignored the legal framework that was already in place to condemn, inquisition, confiscate and sell the estates of Loyalist fugitives. After months of delay, in September, the General Assembly defeated a bill in keeping with the proposal of the petitioners by a resounding six-to-thirty margin, despite the support of all three Monmouth delegates.

Spring 1780: The Articles for Retaliation

By June 1780, Monmouth County's Whigs were fighting a hopeless war on many fronts against Loyalist enemies. From Sandy Hook, Colonel Tye's Black Brigade and other Loyalist raiders conducted a series of devastating raids into eastern Monmouth County. Along the Raritan Bay shore groups of horse and cattle thieves, known as cowboys, were stealing "upwards of 100 horses" from Monmouth farms. Meanwhile, Pine Robber gangs terrorized the southern Monmouth County shore, and entire villages were lured by profits to participate in the London trade.

The desperate conditions drove a large number of Monmouthers toward vigilantism. Colonel David Forman wrote to George Washington, complaining of the raids being made by Loyalist irregulars, and requested permission to "execute prisoners taken that way." That same month, two Monmouth County petitions were read in the state assembly. The first requested "a law may be enacted to enable them to retaliate upon the disaffected in the said County, under proper regulations and restrictions." The second called for empowering the petitioners to "apprehend a number of the most notorious disaffected…and to keep them in close custody until the loyal subjects of the State, in the hands of the refugees are liberated, and that a large body of men be sent to the relief of that county." Concurrently, a group of Monmouth's leaders created the Association for Retaliation. The finished document established the "Articles of Association for Purposes of Retaliation." The preamble of the document states the extreme distress of the authors:

> *Whereas from the frequent incursions and depredations of the Enemy (and more particularly the Refugees) in the county, whereby not only the lives, but the liberty and property of every determined Whig are endangered, They* [the Refugees], *upon every such incursion either burning or destroying houses, making prisoners and most inhumanly treating aged and peaceable inhabitants, and plundering them of all portable property.*

Next, the signers, "actuated solely by the principle of self-preservation," pledged:

> *To hereby solemnly associate for the purposes of Retaliation, and do obligate ourselves to defend such persons as may be appointed to assist this association in the execution thereof; and that we will abide by, and adhere to such rules and regulations, for the purpose of making such retribution to such friends of their country as may hereafter have their houses burned or broke to pieces, their property destroyed or wantonly plundered, their persons made prisoner while peaceably at their own habitations, about lawful business and not under arms.*

These Articles for Retaliation went on to describe the principles upon which the Retaliators would operate. The Retaliators promised to exact equivalent revenge for every kidnapping, burning or other violent act committed against any member of the Association for Retaliation. They empowered a nine-man board of directors to select the most appropriate objects for the retaliatory acts. Because the perpetrators of the raids were generally shielded behind British lines before the Retaliators could act, the directors had the option of selecting self-professed neutrals and others suspected of opposing the Revolution or kin of Loyalist refugees as the proper objects of retaliation:

> *It is a fact notorious to everyone that these depredations have always been committed by the Refugees (either Black or White) that have left this county, or by their influence or procurement; many of whom have near relations and*

friends that have, in general, been suffered to reside unmolested amongst us, numbers of which, we have full reason to believe, are aiding and accessory to those detestable practices.

From the moment of their creation, the Retaliators put themselves on an illegal course. First, the Retaliators empowered themselves to act as their own police force and legal system. Second, the Retaliators decided that relatives of Loyalist refugees or suspected Loyalist sympathizers were viable objects for retaliation even if these individuals could not be concretely linked to Loyalist raids and robberies. Because the Retaliators lacked the military power to strike back at their Loyalist foes on Staten Island and Sandy Hook, they had no choice but to direct most of their efforts against the local disaffected.

The Articles for Retaliation were apparently circulated throughout most of the county, and eventually nearly all of the county's Whig leaders signed them. The association eventually gained 436 signatures, more names than on any other Revolutionary-era document from Monmouth County. Membership was highest in the triangle of neighborhoods that stretched from Freehold northeast to Middletown Point and southeast to Tinton Falls, but Retaliators resided in every part of the county, except the secluded southern township of Stafford. This widespread support proves that, at its genesis, the Association for Retaliation was a truly popular group. Its members were not on the margins of Monmouth County's Whig establishment—the Retaliators, when founded, *were* Monmouth County's Whig establishment.

SUMMER 1780: THE STRUGGLE FOR LEGITIMACY

It is unclear when the Retaliators first became active (though a Loyalist newspaper in New York first noted their existence on July 1, 1780). Throughout their existence, they were a secretive (if not quite secret) organization. Meetings were rarely advertised, and the resolves and proceedings of the board of directors were usually not recorded. Few records of Retaliator activities exist.

However, the Retaliators were active by the middle of 1780. Twice, armed gangs broke into and plundered the home of Samuel Bard, a Shrewsbury physician who was suspected of harboring Loyalist raiders. After the second attack on his home, Bard and his family fled to Staten Island. Soon after,

Joseph Wood, a captured Loyalist raider, was killed under mysterious circumstances near Colts Neck. It is likely that the Retaliators committed other acts that escaped documentation.

Word of the Retaliators reached Philadelphia, where the resident French diplomat, Conrad Alexandre Gerard, wrote:

> *The impunity with which the Tories who lived in New Jersey have exercised all kinds of extortion while under British protection has embittered the Whigs, who have themselves re-assembled throughout all parts of the County of Monmouth, which is very fertile in Tories. They [the Tories] infest their roads with robbery, and the Whigs give hunt. They [the Whigs] seize property all over, where they [the Whigs] drag them [suspected Tories] before juries of their choice and assume the rights of the entire body of people; they [the Whigs] pronounce them guilty and enforce their sentences immediately without due processes, and confiscate their [suspected Tory] goods. People hope that this rage will calm down through publick vengeance and the particular exercises of the Whigs. If such exercises are the good fruits of Democracy, this is a fruit people should not wish on their enemies.*

Once exposed to public scrutiny, the Retaliators attempted to gain legal recognition for their vigilante group. In June 1780, they sent two petitions to the New Jersey legislature hoping to have the Association for Retaliation officially recognized. The petitioners railed against

> *the enemy amongst us, who not only conceal the plunderers, but, we believe, give information as to most of our militia movements, and are so crafty that we are not able to bring lawful accusations against them, although there is great reason to think them active as aforesaid.*

The petitioners warned that the Loyalist raids, "if not fully stopped, will in a short time lay the greatest part of sd. County under the power of the Enemy, to the great destruction of the good subjects of this state." The petitioners concluded that because

> *no means appears to us to be so effective as that of retaliation, we therefore earnestly pray that your Honourable body will form such a law as may enable us to make such retaliation, as person for person and property for property, under such restrictions as your Honours will deem most adequate.*

126

In addition to the petitions, Monmouthers continued to press the New Jersey government for broader local powers, including permitting local officials to take suspected Loyalist sympathizers prisoner in retaliation for kidnappings of Whigs. On June 9, a memorial from Monmouth County proposed that

> *a law may be passed authorizing them* [local officers] *to apprehend a number of the most notorious of the disaffected who are related to the most considerable refugees, and to keep them in close custody until the loyal subjects of this State in the hands of the Refugees are liberated.*

No doubt, the memorialists were hoping that the legislature would at least endorse the principles of retaliation if not necessarily the Association for Retaliation.

The Retaliators did not wait for the New Jersey legislature to finish its deliberations. On July 1, 1780, the Association for Retaliation held its first public meeting. The members reaffirmed their commitment to the association and the principle of retaliation. They also swore to keep the association's orders secret or face the "direst penalty." The Retaliators then held elections and selected David Forman, the most Machiavellian of Monmouth's Whigs, to serve as chairman. A few days later, Forman's friend and fellow Retaliator Nathaniel Scudder wrote to his son:

> *General Forman is our Chairman, & the Association has jointly pledged themselves and their fortunes to support and defend us; you will not doubt that the execution* [of retaliatory acts] *will be rigidly punctual & delivered.*

The decision to turn the Retaliators into a vigilante group under the leadership of a man whose contempt for due process of the law was already widely known produced calamitous results for those Retaliators who had hoped to legitimize the group. Two weeks after the association's July 1 public meeting, Nathaniel Scudder wrote to Henry Laurens, president of the Continental Congress, seeking support for the practice of retaliation. Scudder laid out the distress of Monmouth's Whigs—"We suffer greatly in this part of the Country due to the murder, depredation and kidnappings of the refugees and disaffected"—and then candidly discussed the formation of the Retaliators:

> *We have, from the necessity of our case, on the sole ground of self-preservation, been compelled to enter into a general association for the purpose of Retaliation on the persons and the property of the notoriously disaffected yet residing amongst us for all damages, depredations, burnings, kidnappings &c. done or committed by any of the Refugees upon the Associators in this neighbourhood; We amount to near or quite 500, and the number is daily increasing—They [we] have chosen a Committee of Execution and have solemnly pledged themselves [ourselves] to defend them [us] in the prosecution of business—An eye for an eye & a tooth for a tooth.*

Scudder also addressed the critiques that were already building against the Retaliators:

> *We are well aware of the objections this distressing mode is liable to bring, as being not agreeable to Law, liable to abuse, and likely sometimes to injure the innocent—but alas, my dear friend, necessity has no law; We could no longer consent to be murdered and plundered by rule while from the laxness & timidity & indecision of our own Magistrates, the law is rather a screen for the Tories, while they [legal protections] afford but little security to the well-affected citizens.*

Scudder's letter to Laurens was part of a broader effort to gain acceptance of the Retaliators. On September 17, 1780, in a petition to the New Jersey legislature, the Retaliators explained, "After resolving every scheme that occurred to our imaginations for our protection during the recess of your Honourable houses [in June and July], we finally affixed on an association for the purposes of a well-regulated retaliation." The petitioners made three points. First, the existence of the Association for Retaliation had already produced positive results: "the mere measure of an Association did for a considerable time put a total stop to the practice of plundering & manstealing." Second, the petitioners argued that the disaffected were hoping that the legislature would disavow the Retaliators:

> *They dare that your Honourable Houses would, immediately upon sitting, disapprove the measure, etc., by such means inducing the influential and opulent disaffected to believe that no lasting injury be derived on them on the scheme of Retaliation.*

Finally, the petitioners set out why the disaffected citizens of Monmouth County were deserving targets of retaliation:

First, because they be well affected to the Government of Great Britain, & consequently withhold aid from and conspire to ruin the affairs of this and the other United States. Secondly, because a number of them hold active correspondence and trade with the Enemy to the enriching of themselves and the ruin of the Loyal subjects of this and other States in this Union. Thirdly, because it is a fact notoriously known that those disaffected persons do daily see the plundering parties pass their houses in open daylight on their intended incursions and never give the troops on duty or your Loyal subjects any information on their approaches, but on the contrary, many of them have the plundering refugees in their houses, and will, when enquired of by any of our scouting parties, in a most solemn manner, declare they know nothing of them.

The sixty-nine petitioners included many of Monmouth's high-ranking officeholders and militia officers—Judge Peter Forman, Judge John Anderson, Congressman Nathaniel Scudder, John Covenhoven (one of the writers of the New Jersey Constitution), County Clerk Kenneth Anderson, Reverend John Woodhull, Colonel Samuel Forman, Captain James Green, Captain Kenneth Hankinson, Captain Stephen Fleming and Captain Thomas Chadwick. Interestingly, the Retaliators' controversial chairman, David Forman, did not sign the petition, a reflection of his low standing in the New Jersey legislature.

The September 17 petition was accompanied by the Articles for Retaliation and an appeal from Nathaniel Scudder and Lieutenant Colonel Thomas Henderson to address the New Jersey legislature on behalf of the Association for Retaliation. On September 23, Scudder and Henderson were given an audience before the legislature and allowed to present a memorial "praying that a law may be passed to authorize the well-affected inhabitants to retaliate upon the property of the disaffected of said county." The lower house of the legislature, the assembly, then formed a committee to consider recognizing the Retaliators. Two days later, a petition arrived from Joseph Salter, a well-connected creditor and Dover Township landholder whose son had become a Loyalist. Salter's petition noted that he and John Hartshorne (another large landholder with disaffection in his family) had been recently mistreated by the Retaliators:

> *Captain [James] Green, with a number of men under his command, had forcibly seized and carried away sundry articles of furniture belonging to the said petitioner and to John Hartshorne of the same county, under the pretense of Retaliation; that he had sought redress through the medium of the law without effect.*

Salter's petition proved that the Retaliators were practicing their retaliation while simultaneously petitioning the legislature for permission to practice retaliation.

On September 29, the committee charged with investigating the Association for Retaliation issued a scathing report on the group. The report recognized the desperate situation in Monmouth County and concluded that Governor William Livingston and the legislature should be more "spirited" in assigning militia from other New Jersey counties to help protect Monmouth County. But the report went on to denounce the Retaliators as

> *an illegal and dangerous combination, utterly subversive to the law, highly dangerous to the Government, immediately tending to create disunion among the inhabitants, directly leading toward anarchy and confusion, and tending to the dissolution of the constitution and government.*

The report encouraged the Retaliators to enforce the law through legal means and military service rather than terror, and it concluded that legal means of battling the Loyalist plunderers "would have a much more evident tendency to have produced security for the said county, and safety for the well affected, than any illegal combination whatever." The report was quickly approved by the legislature.

Despite this denunciation, there was some question in the assembly as to whether it had issued an outright prohibition on the Retaliators or merely expressed strong disapproval of the group. For this reason, James Mott, a Monmouth County assemblyman and an early opponent of the Retaliators, proposed adding to the report "that the Association referred to in the memorial ought to be discountenanced by the Legislature as illegal, and contrary to the Laws of this State." Mott probably believed that the report, though harsh in its appraisal of the Retaliators, had not explicitly banned the existence of the group. His amendment backfired on October 2 when the assembly defeated adding the new language to the report by an eleven-to-fourteen vote. This important vote allowed the Retaliators to maintain that the legislature had frowned on their group but had not declared it illegal. The Retaliators were not deterred; in December, another prominent disaffected citizen, Daniel Van Mater, reported being "cruelly and unjustly treated, by having his property clandestinely taken from him" by a gang of Retaliators led by Captain James Green.

The timidity of the New Jersey legislature requires further exploration. As a fledgling government waging a difficult war, the New Jersey government had only limited legitimacy and power. Even if the legislators had voted to declare the Retaliators illegal, the state lacked the means to check the vigilante activity in Monmouth County. While the Retaliators were beyond the bounds of the law, they were still allies in the fight for independence; there was little appetite to take them on. In expressing disapproval for the Retaliators without declaring the group illegal, the New Jersey government was doing all that a weak government could do.

Fall 1780 and 1781:
Opposition on the Homefront

When founded, the Retaliators were an uneasy alliance of moderate and radical Whigs. Though the boundaries between these rival blocs are vague, a few generalizations can be made about the leaders of each faction. The leading moderates—Colonel Asher Holmes, Assemblyman James Mott, Assemblyman Joseph Holmes, Magistrate Peter Schenck, Lieutenant Colonel John Smock, Attorney William Willocks and Assemblyman Hendrick Smock—were generally of Dutch descent, and most resided in Middletown and Shrewsbury Townships. In contrast, Monmouth's leading radicals—David Forman, Colonel Samuel Forman, Nathaniel Scudder, Major Elisha Walton, Lieutenant Colonel Thomas Henderson, Captain Kenneth Hankinson and Captain James Green—were generally Presbyterians who lived near Freehold, the county seat. The factions divided over a citizen's right to legal protection versus the government's need to wage a civil war, with the moderates favoring greater legal protections and the radicals wanting to sacrifice those protections if they interfered with the need to wage war.

As the war dragged into the 1780s, the radicals continued to petition for laws to punish suspected Loyalists and impress private goods to support the war effort, and the moderates continued to oppose any proposed law that did not include legal protections for individuals. It was probably unrealistic to have expected that these factions, which competed every October in the county elections, could peacefully coexist inside a secretive union. When the leaders of both factions signed the Articles for Retaliation, they hoped that their solidarity would awe the Loyalists into relenting in their attacks. When security did not materialize and the Retaliators moved from a paper association to an active vigilante society, Whig unity shattered.

Deprived of political legitimacy and censured for its existence, the Association for Retaliation lost its moderate Whig members in late 1780. It can be safely assumed that many of these moderates were never active. All that was needed was a spark to move the moderates into the role of active opponents of the Retaliators. That spark was provided at the 1780 county elections, held in Freehold on October 10. The elections erupted into controversy when the election judges refused to hold the polls open for a customary second day, effectively preventing full participation from the moderate-leaning voters of Middletown and the shore townships with long journeys to Freehold. The result of the early closure of the polls was that a full slate of radicals—Nathaniel Scudder, Thomas Henderson and Thomas Seabrook—was elected to the legislature. A petition protesting the election noted that James Mott, a moderate candidate for the legislature, was "shamefully beaten and otherwise ill-treated" for protesting the early closure. Court records show that the instigator of the attack was Retaliator chairman David Forman, who pled guilty to assault and confessed that "he did beat, wound and ill-treat" Mott. The election day scandal soured the already tense relations between the moderates and the radicals and probably contributed greatly to the moderates' estrangement from the Retaliators.

The issue of prisoner-of-war exchanges drove a second wedge between the radical and moderate Whigs, especially after the kidnapping of the leading moderate, Hendrick Smock (one of only two moderates on the Retaliator board of directors). On August 22, a small Loyalist raiding party from Sandy Hook slipped past the inadequate militia defenses and captured both Hendrick and John Smock (the third prominent Smock, Captain Barnes Smock, was already a prisoner). Hendrick Smock's association with the Retaliators may have been one of the reasons for his capture: a Loyalist newspaper in New York happily noted that Smock "was of the Associated Community of Retaliators upon the Tories" in its report on the capture.

As was the custom when a militia officer was captured, other militia officers immediately pursued a prisoner exchange with the enemy. Typically, exchanges were carried out by paroling a prisoner to go within enemy lines to negotiate the exchange on behalf of his captors. Colonel Asher Holmes took this course: he paroled captured Loyalist John Williams to go to New York. However, Holmes's action drew censure from the Retaliators. The board of directors of the Association for Retaliation sent a letter, Retaliating Committee Order No. 16, to Asher Holmes—it is apparently the only written order of the Retaliators that still exists. The directors of the Retaliators stated their opposition to paroling prisoners to New York to arrange prisoner exchanges and chastised Holmes for refusing to appear before the Retaliators' board to explain his actions:

> We are sorry to learn of your refusal to attend, after first a verbal request from a member [of the board of directors], and afterward a note from the Chairman [David Forman], without assigning any particular reason. Given the attending members' real concern—we do therefore again request your attendance, or that you assign the particular reason for refusing.

Though reserved in its language, Retaliating Committee Order No. 16 shows the widening split between Monmouth County's Whigs. If Holmes was conducting prisoner exchanges, the Retaliators' policy of eye-for-eye retaliation was compromised.

Retaliating Committee Order No. 16 was only a part of a larger attempt by David Forman and the active Retaliators to curb prisoner exchanges. Weeks earlier Forman sent a letter to George Washington complaining of the militia-sponsored exchanges. Forman blasted the practice as "replete with evil" and concluded that "with every [exchange] made, we give encouragement to that British mode of man-stealing, that once gone into, will always enable them [the enemy] to hold a large ball of prisoners against us." Similar appeals were made to Governor William Livingston. The emotional issue of prisoner exchanges even pushed the New Jersey legislature toward endorsing retaliation. On January 6, 1781, the legislature ordered the state's Commissary of Prisoners to suspend prisoner exchanges and place three enemy prisoners in irons in retaliation for the cruel imprisonment of three Monmouth prisoners, Hendrick Smock, Hendrick Johnson and John Tanner. The three Monmouthers had been placed in irons by Thomas Crowell of the Associated Loyalists (a Monmouth County Loyalist refugee) after Crowell was rebuffed in attempts to arrange a prisoner exchange. Yet the legislature's flirtation with retaliation ended when Clayton Tilton of the Associated Loyalists and Asher Holmes arranged an exchange for the Monmouthers a month later.

By the middle of 1781, most of Monmouth's moderate Whigs were actively working against the Retaliators. On May 10, 1781, a group of moderates formed the Whig Society of Monmouth County. Led by two of Monmouth's elder statesmen, John Covenhoven and William Wilcocks (formerly a judge advocate in the Continental army), the Whig Society was a counterweight to the Retaliators. The Whig Society had a modest agenda: it pledged only to preserve the value of Continental money and boycott the disaffecteds who refused to accept it. While the Articles for Retaliation promised violence and collective action, the Whig Society modestly pledged, "We will use our utmost endeavours to support the paper currency of this state, and to execute the law strictly against every person who shall, to our knowledge, attempt to depreciate it." While Retaliators took extralegal action against perceived enemies for any number of offenses, the Whig Society promised to only expose and boycott those who practiced economic disaffection.

The creation of the rival Whig Society again prompted the Retaliators to seek legal recognition for the policy of retaliation. Within days of the creation of the Whig Society, the Retaliators sent three petitions to the New Jersey legislature praying again for reconsideration of the policy of retaliation. The near identical petitions presented a series of grievances and then asked for permission to practice retaliation. One petition, signed by several leading Retaliators, including David Forman, the Reverend Benjamin DuBois, Kenneth Hankinson and Thomas Henderson, begged "permission to practice retaliation and to have recourse to retaliating upon the disaffected amongst us." The petitioners concluded, "We would therefore pray your Honours pass an act for [the legalization of] all past retaliation, and that you would disenfranchise all amongst us [who are] notoriously disaffected."

The petitions reveal the illegality of the Retaliators, for the petitioners were, in effect, requesting permission to practice policies that had been already disavowed and to continue practices that even the Retaliators acknowledged as extralegal. One of these petitions revealed growing opposition to the Retaliators within Monmouth County. Next to the twenty-five petition signers were ten additional signatures broken off by the phrase, "We agree with the whole petition, excepting the clause concerning Retaliation." Among these ten signers were two probable members of the Whig Society, the merchant Thomas Cox and former Continental army captain Peter Wikoff.

The May 1781 petitions urging the New Jersey legislature to act against the disaffecteds and support retaliation did not stir the lawmakers into action. Several months later, one of Monmouth's delegates to the General Assembly, the Retaliator Thomas Henderson, forced the issue. On October 2, 1781, Henderson introduced a bill entitled "An Act to Procure Reparations to the Loyal Citizens of this State, for Damages They May Sustain from Nocturnal Plunderers." The bill proposed to levy a tax upon disaffected citizens to compensate victims of Loyalist raids. But, like other Retaliator-sponsored ideas, the idea of taxing disaffected persons who had been already punished for past offenses was contrary to due process of the law. Henderson's bill was defeated by a ten-to-nineteen vote, despite the unanimous support of the Monmouth delegation—Henderson, Nathaniel Scudder and Thomas Seabrook, all Retaliators.

Meanwhile, the Retaliators continued their vigilante actions with little regard for the New Jersey legislature. According to three anti-Retaliator petitions sent to the New Jersey Assembly in December 1781, Retaliator abuses reached their most flagrant that year. The petitioners accused the Retaliators of dispatching parties of armed men to victimize innocent people, "some they have imprisoned, from some they have taken goods & others money." The petitioners also argued that because Retaliators held some offices and coerced other officeholders, there was no legal recourse. "When those injured persons have attempted to right themselves by law," the petitioners stated, "they have been abused, their lives threatened and some unmercifully beaten by those persons who have taken their property; officers of the law have been prevented from doing their duty, & threatened for attempting it." In addition, the petitioners noted the outrageous conduct of the Retaliators at the October 1781 elections:

At the late election, a number of men (some in arms) appeared in a hostile manner, threatening all such persons as they called Tories or [London] Traders if they should vote; a writing was put up at the Court House to the same effect; several persons were inhumanly beaten, some of them after they had voted, and some of them drove away who were legally entitled to vote, and went away without voting not thinking themselves safe, as they [the Retaliators] did not confine their abuse to people they judged disaffected, but beat and abused several, and at the close of the election, one of the inspectors was attacked going down the stairs and most barbarously beaten.

In the strong, sweeping language usually reserved for Loyalist refugees, the petitioners charged the Retaliators with "corrupting the morals of the people & encouraging many others to plunder for their own gain, and committing other crimes with impunity." The petitioners concluded by labeling the Retaliators "a combination to trample all law underfoot."

The signatures on the three anti-Retaliator petitions prove that the Retaliators spurred an alliance between Monmouth's moderate Whigs and the disaffected still participating in government. Most of the sixty-eight anti-Retaliator petitioners were shore residents and Quakers with little affection for the new government. Many were, no doubt, victims or kin to victims of Retaliator abuses. But these petitions also contain the signatures of a number of important moderate Whigs, including two magistrates, Abiel Aiken and Peter Schenck; two former New Jersey assemblymen, James Mott and Joseph Holmes; and two kin of prominent Retaliators, Lewis Forman and John Chadwick. By the end of 1781, the radical course of the Retaliators had driven an insurmountable wedge between Monmouth's radical and moderate Whigs—and pushed the moderates into an alliance with the disaffecteds.

1782: CLIMACTIC RETALIATION

By 1782, the American Revolution, as a military event, was essentially over. The British army barricaded itself in New York City, and the British navy left North America to battle European enemies in other parts of the British Empire. Throughout the rebelling colonies, Loyalists were either subdued or sheltered behind British lines in New York. Even the military frontier surrounding New York City was quieter. But there were exceptions to the cease-fire, and one of the most glaring exceptions was Monmouth County, which hosted more raids and skirmishes in 1782 than in all the other New Jersey counties combined.

The continued violence in Monmouth County had many causes, including the continued British presence on the Sandy Hook peninsula and disaffection in the shore townships. But the largest single reason for the continued violence in Monmouth County were the provocations of the Retaliators and the equal provocations of their Loyalist foes, now under guidance of the Board of Associated Loyalists (a Loyalist organization that also practiced retaliation). Chartered in late 1780, the Associated Loyalists were created by a faction of Loyalist refugees in New York who believed the British war effort lacked energy and a necessary punitive strategy. Under the leadership of New Jersey's last royal governor, William Franklin, the Associated Loyalists claimed five hundred members, though their effective strength on any given day was probably much lower.

The enmity between the Retaliators and the Associated Loyalists was direct; four of the Associated Loyalists' company commanders were Monmouth County refugees—Joseph Allen, Clayton Tilton, Thomas Crowell and Richard Lippincott—and all four led incursions into Monmouth County. The antipathy was further stoked by David Forman's election as a judge of the Monmouth County Courts and the capital convictions of numerous Loyalists. The Board of Associated Loyalists became so enraged with David Forman that it authorized a raid against Freehold in March 1782 with the goals of freeing the prisoners in the Monmouth jail and capturing him.

The Retaliators were similarly aware of the Associated Loyalists. In December 1781, when the New Jersey legislature denounced the Associated Loyalists in a report to the Continental Congress, it was Thomas Henderson, a leading Retaliator, who wrote the report. Henderson characterized the Associated Loyalists as illegal, ungoverned by military convention and motivated solely by revenge (the same arguments had been made about the Retaliators). The report labeled the Associated Loyalists a "new fangled body of executioners" that existed "for the express purpose of plundering and destroying the well-affected inhabitants, and of kidnapping the most active defenders of our country." The report concluded with confidential advice for the New Jersey delegates at Congress. They were instructed not to tolerate "any empty declarations of purposes never to be executed" and to lobby for a policy of retaliation "so that the vengeance of an injured people may fall on British officers and others whose influence may induce the British Commander and Chief to do justice to the citizens of this State." New Jerseyians were frustrated by Congress's inaction following its October 1 statement that it would "cause exemplary retaliation to be executed on the enemy for all acts of cruelty committed by them against the citizens and inhabitants of these states." Henderson personally delivered the report to the Continental Congress.

In 1782, as the war cooled down in other areas, the conflict between the Retaliators and the Associated Loyalists continued to escalate. Both groups believed that the only way to curb the abuses of the opposition was to commit retaliatory acts, stoking the cycle of continued violence.

On March 30, 1782, a party of state troops near Long Branch captured a small party of Associated Loyalists that included the veteran raider Philip White (two years earlier, White had participated in a raid in which the Whig John Russell was murdered in his house). The Loyalists were disarmed and marched back toward the Monmouth County jail at Freehold. But this routine event took a strange turn when the state troops gave custody of one of the prisoners—Philip White—over to John Russell Jr., John North and William Borden. The three new guards separated White from the other prisoners and provoked him to attempt an escape. When White ran, the three mounted guards hunted him down and murdered him. The intentions of the guards are betrayed by the unusual circumstances of White's demise, including multiple sword wounds to the head and body before he was ultimately killed.

White's murder prompted the Associated Loyalists to strike back. Two weeks later, Captain Joshua Huddy of Monmouth County (who had been captured during an Associated Loyalist raid on Toms River three weeks earlier) was taken out of jail, brought back into Monmouth County and hanged by an Associated Loyalist party under Captain Richard Lippincott, a Monmouth County refugee. Huddy was infamous to the Loyalists because of his role in hanging the Loyalist Stephen Edwards early in the war. Huddy's corpse was left swinging with a note pinned to his chest proclaiming the murder an act of revenge for White's murder and promising further retaliation:

> We, the Refugees, having long beheld with grief the cruel murders of our brethren, and finding nothing but such measures daily carried into execution; we therefore determine not to suffer without taking vengeance for the numerous cruelties, and thus begin, having made use of Captain Huddy as the first object to present to your view, and determine to hang man for man while there is a refugee still existing. Up goes Huddy for Phil. White.

Shortly afterward, the Board of the Associated Loyalists defended their action by calling attention to "a sett [sic] of vindictive rebels well known by the designation Monmouth Retaliators." The Loyalists were "fired" to seek revenge because they had "beheld many of their friends and neighbors butchered in cold blood." Without apology the Associated Loyalists stated, "We thought it high time to convince the rebels we would no longer tamely submit to such glaring acts of barbarity."

This note pinned to Huddy and the letter from the Board of Associated Loyalists show the remarkably similar postures of the Associated Loyalists and the Retaliators: with only a few minor changes, these documents easily could have been written by the Retaliators about the Associated Loyalists. The similarity between the Associated Loyalists and Retaliators was not lost on General Guy Carleton, the newly installed British commander in chief in New York who wrote to Washington in May 1782 that "the same spirit of revenge has mutually animated the people of New Jersey and the Refugees under my command, [both] are equally criminal and deserving punishment." An anonymous New Jersey memorialist expressed similar sentiments to the New Jersey legislature, noting "the enemy, I fear with good ground, are compelled to retaliate" due to Whig provocations, including vindictive raids against Loyalists on Staten Island. The so-called Huddy Affair caused a diplomatic bonfire that nearly prompted General Washington to hang a British officer, Captain Charles Asgill, and briefly threatened the Paris peace talks.

The furor of the Huddy Affair prompted the Retaliators to seek legal recognition for the policy of retaliation one last time. On May 25, 1782, a Monmouth County petition was sent to the legislature, praying that "an act may be passed for levying the damages sustained from the Refugees by tax upon the disaffected, and for indemnification of those persons who have seized property by virtue of an association entered in sd. County for Retaliation." But this petition was countered by a set of anti-Retaliator petitions that arrived on the same day. On May 31, the General Assembly voted to disavow the pro-retaliation petition by a twenty-three-to-eight margin.

Despite continued rebuffs in the legislature, the Retaliators continued to act. In May and June 1782, Forman, serving as a judge of the court of common pleas, used his office to issue orders instructing militia officers to impress the horses of up to eight suspected but uncharged Loyalist sympathizers. A few months later, sixty-nine Retaliator victims petitioned the New Jersey legislature. The petitioners defended themselves as "peaceable inhabitants of the State who have always contributed their proportion to the support of the government, and are at all times amenable to the laws." Next they described the abuses committed "by order of a body of men, who title themselves the Association for Retaliation." The petitioners pleaded:

Our doors have been forced open, our houses rifled of our beds and other furniture, our stock drove away, and our teams broken up. We have been deprived of all means of tilling our land and many of us, who lived in a degree of affluence, now find it difficult to procure sustenance for our families.

The exasperation of the petitioners brought about a harsh appraisal of legal protections in Monmouth County.

We have no form of tryal [sic]; if any crimes are layed [sic] to our charge, we have no chance of defending ourselves, nor any account of how our property, thus torn away, is disposed of. Tho' diverse of us have been imprisoned, and one [Squire John Taylor] for months confined in the common gaol, in the course of which time a Court of Oyer and Terminer was held over his head—writs of habeas corpus have been disregarded by the Sheriff. In short, every attempt at recourse by the law has been of no effect, owing, as we firmly believe, to the prevailing influence of sd. Association.

The petitioners closed by specifically naming David Forman as responsible for many of the abuses and calling for his removal as justice of the courts.

The continued troubles in Monmouth County finally prompted the New Jersey legislature to action. On September 25, the legislature appointed a committee to consider censuring the Retaliators and to review "sundry petitions from a number of inhabitants of the County of Monmouth, complaining of the conduct of David Forman, First Judge of the Court of Common Pleas in the County of Monmouth." Hearings into Forman's conduct were held on November 19 and 20, and on November 21 the assembly held three votes concerning Forman. First, the assembly unanimously voted to void the warrants Forman had issued to impress the horses of the eight suspected Loyalist sympathizers. Second, the assembly narrowly passed (sixteen to thirteen) a resolution denouncing Forman for simultaneously serving as judge of the court and chairman of the Association for Retaliation. However, the assembly showed its timidity in the third vote. By a twelve-to-seventeen margin, it failed to pass a resolution to impeach Forman and remove him from office. As in 1780, the New Jersey Assembly had declared its distaste for the Retaliators and their brutal actions but stopped short of taking decisive action that might force a confrontation with the group.

1783: DISSOLUTION

The Retaliators stayed active into 1783; in March, they advertised in the *New Jersey Gazette* a general meeting for all members. The group's violent intentions remained unchanged, thinly hidden behind warnings that the Retaliators needed "to be prepared for future depredations." Perhaps because of pressure from the New Jersey government, David Forman resigned as chairman and was replaced by Captain Kenneth Hankinson, a militia officer with a record of scandal and radicalism. Forman's departure, the dissolution of the rival Associated Loyalists and the cessation of Loyalist raids led to a general slowdown in Retaliator activities; however, those activities still did not cease.

In July 1783, three sailors from the HMS *Vixen*, stationed at Sandy Hook, went on a routine trip to the freshwater well at the bottom of the Hook. There, a gang of Retaliators captured and severely beat them. The gang then released one of the sailors to go back to the ship and give testimony of the Retaliators' vigilance. After the incident, Lieutenant John White of the *Vixen* took the highly unusual step of writing directly to David Forman. "I am confident that you would never give sanction to such an affair," White flattered Forman. But White then issued a blunt caution: he warned Forman that the offenders must be punished "to prevent retaliations that might be the consequence of such unwarrantable proceedings." There is no evidence that the offenders were brought to justice or that White acted on his threat.

By the end of 1783, the Retaliators had faded into inactivity. The war was over, and their reason to exist—to punish Loyalist raiders and sympathizers—expired with the Loyalist evacuations from New York. Though individual Monmouthers continued to hunt down and beat suspected Loyalists well into the postwar period, these events were sporadic and uncoordinated. The demise of the Retaliators may also have been hastened by the rise of a new association in 1783: the Association to Oppose the Return of Tories. This association pledged to oppose any effort to reintegrate Loyalists into society, but it also pledged to conduct its affairs legally. Signed by more than two hundred Monmouthers, including Sheriff John Burrowes and many less prominent Retaliators, the Association to Oppose the Return of Tories gave radical Whigs a less violent option than the Retaliators, though the exact relationship between these groups is impossible to discern from surviving documents.

CONCLUSION

The Retaliators came into existence as a self-defense pact, and acts of vengeance were only an unfortunate tactic for achieving an important goal—security for vulnerable people along the military frontier. But the Retaliators did little to support or enhance the military defenses of Monmouth County. Most leading Retaliators—David Forman, Thomas Henderson, Nathaniel Scudder and Thomas Seabrook (all high-ranking military officers early in the war)—dropped out of the military during the later years of the war. Perhaps they deemed Retaliator business more important, or perhaps they concluded that the militia was an ineffective check on Loyalist raids. Relations with moderate Whigs had also soured to the point that most leading Retaliators probably felt unwelcome in a militia led by Colonel Asher Holmes, a Retaliator foe. Whatever the reason, the Retaliators were a drag on their county's military resources.

The failure of the Retaliators as a self-defense entity partially explains why similar vigilante societies did not spread throughout New Jersey, but it does little to explain why the Retaliators took root in Monmouth County in the first place. The Retaliator movement found fertile soil in Monmouth County partly because the county was the scene of pervasive civil warfare, but other locales, such as Bergen County, New Jersey, were also ravaged by civil warfare, especially early in the war. Apparently, Monmouth County was unique in two important ways. First, while Whigs gradually gained the upper hand in the other civil wars around New York City, Monmouth County's civil war remained stalemated into the 1780s—creating extraordinary Whig frustration inside the county. Second, Monmouth County, for reasons that remain unclear, produced an inordinately large number of unprincipled, Machiavellian leaders. David Forman and the leaders of the county's radical Whig bloc were guilty of far more than vigilantism during the war. They coerced elections, manipulated the legal system, rigged the auctions of confiscated Loyalist estates, engaged in a series of collusive privateering and salt-making ventures and perpetrated an unending string of harassments against perceived enemies throughout. Abuses like these were not unique to Monmouth County, but the sheer quantity of such scandalous events in Monmouth County stands out. In this context, the vigilantism and brutality of the Retaliators was only part of a collection of distasteful behaviors practiced by Monmouth's radical Whigs.

"A Combination to Trample All Law Underfoot"

For decades, the narrative of the American Revolution was rather simple: in defense of liberty virtuous Whigs took up arms against an oppressive British government. Yet the case of the Retaliators shows that the Whigs were not uniformly virtuous and were, in this instance, deliberately brutal. The existence of the Retaliators should not cast a shadow over the lofty ideals of the Revolution or diminish the genuine heroism of many Whigs. Nor should Retaliator actions redeem the Loyalist refugees, whose increasingly vindictive raids across the military frontier, by 1782, were even disliked by the British. Rather, the infamous tenure of the Retaliators and their Associated Loyalist foes demonstrates that desperate people are prone to act desperately, and any conflict that plunges thousands of people into seven years of civil warfare will inevitably produce a great many thugs on both sides, regardless of the merit of the larger cause.

This chapter is based on an essay of the same name that appeared in the journal New Jersey History *in 1997, though it has been considerably modified and updated.*

CONCLUDING THOUGHTS AND FURTHER READING

CONCLUDING THOUGHTS

While Monmouth County was a part of the military frontier that stretched around British-held New York City, it was also unique. The civil warfare that occurred there was longer lasting and probably more brutal than elsewhere in the New York City theatre. There are a few reasons for this:

1. The British naval base at Sandy Hook gave Loyalists a more convenient depot for selling booty, receiving war materials and receiving temporary refuge. No other piece of New Jersey was occupied by the British continuously through the war.
2. The Pine Robber gangs of the lower shore found ample lairs in sparsely populated swamps and coves and were supported by disaffected shore villages. They were never conclusively defeated, though their most visible leaders did meet a bloody end.
3. The Retaliators maintained a cycle of retributive violence with Loyalist foes in New York and practiced terror against disaffected and alleged disaffected locals. These "hot" Whigs prevented tensions from "cooling" in Monmouth County, even as the war ebbed elsewhere.

The national-level politics of the Continental Congress and British government only indirectly impacted the war in Monmouth County.

Congress made numerous pronouncements about curbing illegal trade and more effectively protecting military frontier areas, but it lacked the means to carry out its promises. Local Whigs used congressional resolves to support their positions when convenient but proceeded in their actions with or without legal cover. The British government mattered more to the people of Monmouth County because a few of its decisions (i.e., establishing, however briefly, a Loyalist government in Monmouth County, granting freedom to runaway slaves and supporting Loyalist irregulars) primed the pump of local civil warfare. But even among the Loyalists, the most active and dangerous—such as the Associated Loyalists, the Black Brigade and the Pine Robbers—operated outside British control.

State government mattered more than national government: Monmouthers petitioned the state government several dozen times during the war years; Monmouthers believed the state had a responsibility to hear and respond to their concerns. Similarly, Monmouthers demonstrated great passions at the county elections each year, suggesting that they believed that their representatives in state government were very important. But while Governor Livingston was clearly interested in supporting the war effort in military frontier counties, and Monmouth in particular, and the New Jersey legislature was frequently interested in curbing both the London trade and the worst excesses of Monmouth's Whigs, the ability of the state to effectively intervene was generally disappointing. Militia call-ups from other counties rarely delivered the promised support, and only rarely did the state government go beyond reprimand in curbing the worst conduct of Monmouth's radical Whigs.

In this way, the American Revolution in Monmouth County (and many other military frontier localities) resembles the quagmires we see in some parts of the world today where civil warfare continues year after year without end. Ultimately, the outcome of Monmouth County's local war was a happy one, but it was achieved at a tremendous cost and principally because the British chose to undercut their Loyalist allies after the defeat at Yorktown. Without that critical action, it is not clear when (or even if) local Whigs could have brought normalcy to this particularly distressed part of the military frontier.

Further Reading

It is hoped that this book will pique the interest of readers in the American Revolution in New Jersey, but with less focus on George Washington and the campaigns of the great armies and more focus on the seven years of withering local civil warfare that occurred.

For readers who want to explore the civil war theme further, there are several excellent books. Carol Karels's *The American Revolution in Bergen County* (Charleston, SC: The History Press, 2008) is a fine starting point for learning about the American Revolution in northern New Jersey. Although fifty years old, Arthur Pierce's *Smuggler's Wood* (New Brunswick, NJ: Rutgers University Press, 1961) is the most complete overview of the American Revolution along the southern New Jersey shore. Even older but still a very good overview of the American Revolution in New Jersey is Leonard Lundin's *Cockpit of the Revolution: The American Revolution in New Jersey* (Princeton, NJ: Princeton University Press, 1940). An excellent recent study of colonial New Jersey is Brendon McConville's *These Daring Disturbers of the Peace* (Ithaca, NY: Cornell University Press, 2007). Also worth seeking out (and widely available in New Jersey libraries) is the booklet series *New Jersey's Revolutionary War Experience* (Trenton: New Jersey Historical Commission, 1975). On a scholarly level, two highly recommended books are Barbara Mitnick's essay collection, *The American Revolution in New Jersey* (New Brunswick, NJ: Rutgers University Press, 2008), and Peter Wacker's *Land and People: The Cultural Geography of Pre-Industrial New Jersey* (Trenton: New Jersey Historical Commission, 1975). Finally, two books without an explicit New Jersey focus, Harry Ward's *Between the Lines* (Westport, CT: Preager, 2003) and Judith Van Buskirk's *Generous Enemies* (Philadelphia: University of Pennsylvania Press, 2002), contain a great deal of information on the war in New Jersey packaged within well-written and researched larger studies.

Specific to Monmouth County, there is a small body of excellent work. The county's most famous Revolutionary War event, the Battle of Monmouth, is particularly well documented. Recommended are David Martin's *The Philadelphia Campaign: June 1777–July 1778* (Conshohocken, PA: Combined Books, 1993), Samuel Smith's *The Battle of Monmouth* (Monmouth Beach, NJ: Phillip Freneau Press, 1964) and Theodore Thayer's *The Making of a Scapegoat: Washington and Lee at Monmouth* (Port Washington, NY: Kennikat Press, 1976), though a half dozen other works could be just as easily recommended. David Fowler's "Egregious Villains" (PhD diss., Rutgers University, 1987) is the defining work on the Pine Robbers. Another PhD dissertation worth seeking for its discussion of the American Revolution's impact on everyday life is Dennis Ryan's "Six Towns" (New York University, 1974). Two of Ryan's six studied towns are Middletown and Shrewsbury.

A few other local Revolutionary War events are well studied. The hanging of Joshua Huddy and court-martial of his executioner, Richard Lippincott, have been well chronicled by L. Kinvin Wroth in Howard Peckham's *Sources of the American Revolution* (Chicago: Caxton Club, 1978) and Larry Bowman's "The Court Martial of Captain Richard Lippincott" in *New Jersey History* 89 (1979). The precedent-setting case of *Holmes v. Walton* is expertly dissected by the legal historian Philip Hamburger in *Law and Judicial Duty* (Cambridge, MA: Harvard University Press, 2008), and the relevant legal documents from that case have been compiled and transcribed by Paul Axel Lute and posted on the Internet at http://njlegallib.rutgers.edu/hw. Todd Braisted has compiled and posted several very interesting documents related to New Jersey's Loyalists, including Monmouth Loyalists, at www.royalprovincial. com. Finally, there is a good article on the Continental army's flirtation with London trading via Captain Nathaniel Bowman's mission to Manasquan in John U. Rees, "'The Great Distress of the Army for Want of Blankets': Supply Shortages, Suffering Soldiers, and a Secret Mission During the Hard Winter of 1780," *Military Collector & Historian* 52 (Fall 2000).

There are also my previously published works, including: "Factions, Contraband, and Civil War: The Historical Context of *Holmes v. Walton*," in Paul Axel Lute, ed., *"Holmes v. Walton"* (Rutgers University Center for Law & Justice, http://njlegallib.rutgers.edu/hw, February 2010); "An Evenly Balanced County: The Scope and Severity of Civil Warfare in Revolutionary Monmouth County New Jersey," *Journal of Military History* 73, no. 1 (January 2009); "'I Am as Innocent as an Unborn Child': The Loyalism of Edward and George Taylor," *New Jersey History* 123, no. 1 (Spring 2005); "'A Combination to Trample All Law Underfoot': The Association for Retaliation and the American Revolution in Monmouth County, New Jersey," *New Jersey History* 115, no. 3 (1997); *The Allen House Massacre: Establishing the Credibility of a Letter to Determine Historical Fact* (Freehold, NJ: Monmouth County Historical Association, 1996); "'They Do Rather More Harm than Good': Continental Soldiers in Revolutionary Monmouth County," in *Impact: Papers Presented at a Symposium on the Impact of the War of Independence on the Civilian Population* (Morristown, NJ: The Washington Association, 1995); "'So Dangerous a Quarter': The Sandy Hook Lighthouse During the American Revolution," *Keeper's Log, Journal of the United States Lighthouse Society* 44 (Spring 1995); "Revolutionary Times" (quarterly column), *Monmouth County Historical Association Newsletter*, 1994–97; *The Roster of the People of Revolutionary Monmouth County* (Baltimore: Clearfield, 1998); and *The American Revolution in Monmouth*

County: An Annotated Bibliography (Freehold, NJ: Monmouth County Historical Assoc., 1995).

It was not possible to cover every interesting and important topic about the American Revolution in Monmouth County in this book. The most glaring omissions are those related to the Revolutionary War along the shore—Pine Robbers, salt making, privateering, the rivalry between the shore residents and inland residents and the transformation of the Jersey Shore region started by the Revolution. Nor does the book explore the impact of the war on everyday life in Monmouth County or the life of the Loyalists who left the county, either during the war years or afterward. I hope to explore these topics in a later book.

In the interest of keeping this book affordable, the footnotes, which collectively cover more than thirty pages, have been removed. They are on file at the library of the Monmouth County Historical Association (MCHA) in Freehold, New Jersey, where they can be reviewed for a nominal admission fee. The MCHA Library also holds my biographical file, extracts of my database and copies of my previous publications on the American Revolution in Monmouth County. The MCHA Library will mail copies of the notes for a modest fee upon request. Interested individuals should contact the library at library@monmouthhistory.org or 70 Court Street, Freehold, NJ 07728. I am interested in anything that will increase my knowledge of civil warfare during the American Revolution, and Monmouth County in particular. You are welcome to contact me through my website, www.michaeladelberg.com, where you can also learn about my other writings and interests.

INDEX

About the Author

Michael Adelberg has been researching the American Revolution in Monmouth County for more than twenty years. His essays on the American Revolution have appeared in academic journals like the *Journal of Military History* and historical magazines such as the *Keeper's Log*. His research has been the subject of articles in thought journals like the *Wilson Quarterly* and the Jersey Shore's leading newspaper, the *Asbury Park Press*. He is a book reviewer for the *New York Journal of Books*, and his first novel, *The Thinking Man's Bully*, will be published in 2011. Adelberg holds master's degrees in history and public policy and lives with his family in Vienna, Virginia. To learn more about the author and his publications, visit www.michaeladelberg.com.

Visit us at
www.historypress.net
....
This title is also available as an e-book